Run

Different
RACE

Running a Different RACE

SONIA HENRY

RUNNING A DIFFERENT RACE

Printed in Canada

ISBN: 978-1-4866-1326-7

Word Alive Press
131 Cordite Road, Winnipeg, MB R3W 1S1
www.wordalivepress.ca

WORD ALIVE PRESS

RECYCLED
Paper made from recycled material
FSC® C103567

Cataloguing in Publication may be obtained through Library and Archives Canada

Contents

Dedication and Thanks

I dedicate this book to my husband, Elvis. He is a great encourager in the Lord. He is also affectionately called "my beloved" and "Mr. Henry." God has used him to teach me how to love.

I also dedicate the book to my two sons, Jamaal and Jonathan. I thank God for giving them to me so I could acquire the skills of motherhood.

There are some very special individuals I would like to thank for the roles they played and the encouragements they offered in their endeavour to push me onward. I thank my mom, Cislyn. She is my God-ordained mom. When God gives gifts, He is sure to select the best gift for you—and my mom is a gift. Not many individuals can say they remember the day they met their mom, but I can say that. It was a joyous day. To mom, I say thank you very much for the values you have instilled in me and all the hours you spent listening and inspiring me.

To my friend Carlette, who supported me by praying and then calling to say, "Sonia, the book. It's time for the book."

To Pastor Innis, who drove me to get going page by page. He was so happy with the progress, even when I was only able to produce half a page. He poured out words of encouragement.

To my friend Pastor Sharon, who continuously reminded me that God has deposited His words in me and I should speak what He tells me to speak.

To Pastor Suzy, who mentored me with prayer and encouragement. When she didn't have enough words, a book or a CD showed up in the mail.

There are many others who should receive a thank-you note, but I don't have enough pages to do so. You know who you are and I thank you all for your ongoing motivation and encouragement.

Introduction

It is my hope that as you read these writings, they will invoke a new passion in you and bring a great desire and awareness of the voice and presence of God in your life and heart, so you will be stirred to press forward with heightened focus and a steadfast vision.

I pray that as you approach the finish line of your race, you will not be swayed to the left or the right but stay persistent to achieve the goal.

My desire is that as you read about the experiences and encounters I had with my Lord and Saviour, Jesus Christ, through dreams, visions, and real-life situations, you will be encouraged to stir up the gifts He has deposited in you.

Truly, it is His promise to unveil the plans He has for you, plans to give you hope and a future (Jeremiah 29:11). His desire is for you to be who He has made you to be.

I pray that your eyes will see new visions and that you will experience dreams as you fix your mind on Christ.

I pray that God will awaken your ears, and they will be tuned to His still, small voice.

I pray that your heart will become the vessel and temple wherein His presence may dwell (1 Corinthians 6:19).

I pray that as you move forward on your journey, you will become acquainted with His unseen presence.

For His glory!

Part I

True Identity

Into Your presence, You draw me.
Into Your courts of praise.
Into Your presence, You lead me,
Where I may seek Your face.
—Sonia Henry, 2000

1

Desire of My Heart

Not sure where to begin. However, I am writing so I can release the pressure accumulating in my heart. I believe the words will find a suitable place on paper. My pen will finally discover its usefulness—so I begin.

My true heart's desire is to see women as a great army, marching toward their goal and the destiny God has charted out and predestined for their lives. That desire has been in my heart like a little seed since I was a child of about five years. I didn't fully understand it then. As time went on, that seed enlarged and developed into an overwhelming desire to teach. I wanted to teach others to read and write.

My ongoing motivation has been the fact that my father was unable to read or write. He wasn't even able to make the first character in his name, though he attempted many times; he would simply break out in sweats. It was very painful to watch. He passed away at the age of eighty-seven, still unable to read or write. He experienced defeat in that sense. But he was victorious because his heart was captivated by the love of God.

Please, join me as we travel together on this journey. It's a journey through which you may laugh, or you may cry; you may even want to take me by the shoulders, shake me up, and say,

"Girl, what have you...? Why have you...? How have you...?" And so on. I don't want to put words in your mouth.

Most of all, I pray that you will be encouraged. Enjoy the journey.

2

Be Strong and Take Courage

I would like to encourage those in my generation—the boomers—because there are some of us who believe that we've done it all, experienced it all, and now come to the end of the journey.

It is not the end of the journey.

It is, in fact, the beginning of the journey.

There is a sound that is about to be released and you, boomers, are familiar with that sound.

It is the sound of trumpets.

It is the sound of the beginning of battle.

Put on your strength and be made ready, for you are part of a great and mighty army.

Do not be afraid. Be strong. Take courage.

We must be available to make a *booming* declaration for the advancement of the Kingdom of God.

Listen to His voice. He is still speaking.

3

A Gentle Reminder

In the process of writing this book, God gently reminded me of all the words and promises He has spoken to me, of the dreams and visions that have served as insight and foreknowledge, and of the day-to-day occurrences that appeared impossible, yet they were worked out supernaturally.

A number of the dreams and visions have, in reality, been accomplished and evolved. For others, I wait in anticipation for their completion. I thank my Father for allowing me to come to this point in my life, for He extends His hand of grace, mercy, and tenderness as He displays His love for me.

4

The Dream of God

I have learned that the dream of God, once received, remains alive until it is fulfilled or accomplished. The dream will remain in your heart and mind, although sometimes it will appear that it is no longer there. I describe it as "the sleeping dream."

Often, someone will say something to you and it will awake the dream or activate it. In my experience, it doesn't mean that the dream is activated because it is about to come to pass—although that could be the case; it simply means that the dream is still alive, and God is reminding you that He has not forgotten His word to you.

A dream is like a promise from God, and when He gives it to you, He will complete it so He can get the glory. There is a great promise in Isaiah 55:10–11 that says,

> *The rain and snow come down from the heavens and stay on the ground to water the earth. They cause the grain to grow, producing seed for the farmer and bread for the hungry. It is the same with my word. I send it out, and it always produces fruit. It will accomplish all I want it to, and it will prosper everywhere I send it. (NLT)*

The next time you have a dream and know in your heart that it is from God, treat it like a seed planted in deep, rich soil. You will see the result in the season for which it has been predestined. All you have to do is watch and wait.

5

The Unexpected Reflection

I stood in front of the mirror adjusting the beige shopping-day dress I had selected. Despite the fact that it was windy that morning, I maintained my desire to wear the dress. I had made my selection of shoes and purse the day before.

I was excited to go shopping with my beloved. He was already dressed and ready to go. He was usually ready before I was and he would go and sit in the car. I attempted to speed up the process of getting ready.

Ten minutes must have passed because my beloved came back into the house. He said nothing; he only stood by the door. He must have heard the rustling of my items and products on the bathroom counter, so he waited. I didn't want him to change his mind about shopping. I was trying to find complementary attire that would go with my dress.

Finally, I was ready, and my beloved was still standing by the door. He had brought the car very close, so I wouldn't have to endure the wind messing my hair, my dress, and so on. I was grateful for the concern he demonstrated.

We arrived at the shopping mall and still I didn't need to worry about the wind because he located an underground parking lot. We took an elevator to the first shopping level of the mall.

Immediately as we exited the elevator, I saw a mirror. It reached from the ceiling to floor—it was, in fact, massive. I simply couldn't help myself; I took a glance because I wanted to confirm that my beige shopping-day dress was still intact.

I didn't see myself in the mirror. I saw someone else.

I took a glance backward over my shoulder, checking to see if there was another mirror on the opposite wall, one that might reveal an unexpected reflection from the mirror currently facing me.

There was no other.

That's a little bit odd, I thought.

My beloved just kept walking, so he wasn't aware that I was having issues with the mirror. Or perhaps it was the mirror having issues with me.

I didn't want to deal with a fake mirror, so I walked away. Immediately, I felt pressed that I needed to go back and face the mirror.

The reflection still didn't look right. I knew that my dress was beige, but the dress I saw in the mirror was blue. Beautiful. Extremely beautiful blue.

It wasn't a colour that my eyes had ever seen before.

I looked at the image more intensely, from top to bottom.

The reflection wasn't wearing a dress. It was a full-length robe that even covered the shoes. I must have glanced in the mirror three times.

I heard a voice inside me saying, *"I have clothed you in this garment. You don't see yourself the way I see you. It is how I see you."*

I knew it was the Lord; the King of Kings had just clothed me in a royal robe!

I began to walk away from the mirror to join my beloved so we could continue with our shopping. I couldn't just walk; I started skipping like a happy five-year-old heading off to play. My heart was delighted.

The dream ended.

Unable to go back to sleep, I stayed awake for a while as I pondered the dream I'd just had. It was almost overwhelming. Many of the dreams that are given by God are overwhelming. When we find ourselves in the place of awe, we can simply ponder the dream in our hearts.

Finally, I began to pray and asked the Lord why my beloved had not seen what had just happened. Why had he just walked away? Why hadn't he stopped to observe his image in the mirror? After all the questions, the answer came: "*Your beloved is already aware of who he is. I want to show you who you are in My eyes.*"

I'm glad it was not a work day. I was able to linger under the echoes of His voice. The voice was moving in and around my spirit like a soft mist.

The Lord clothes us with garments of authority, so when we're not able to identify who we are in our own eyes, He reveals to us who we are in His eyes.

6

The True Mirror

Usually when I go shopping to purchase articles of clothing, I prefer to select a fitting room equipped with a mirror. If the room doesn't have a mirror, the sales associate may inform me where to locate the nearest one. That advice may be the determining factor in whether I purchase the garment or not.

At one store, I noticed that there were no mirrors in any of the change rooms. I asked a sales associate about this. She explained, "The mirror outside the room provides the right judgment of what you look like in the clothes you try on. It reflects the way others will see you. The mirror in the change room doesn't always tell the truth; it can somewhat distort the appearance of the clothes on the clients and then discourage them from buying the items."

Sales associates will anticipate providing feedback on your appearance. They will desire to provide a compliment, a non-biased indication of whether the garment is suited to your personality.

The Word of God is like a mirror that works in our lives in a similar way. As we read His Word on a daily basis, it shines a light on what is inside us. His Word is like a mirror that seeks out and reflects the inner chambers of our hearts, and it displays what we look like in the eyes of those we interact with regularly.

Our actions and speech is a true reflection of the Word transforming our lives.

In 2 Corinthians 3:18, we read,

> *But we all, with unveiled face, beholding as in a mirror the glory of the Lord, are being transformed into the same image from glory to glory, just as by the Spirit of the Lord.*

In other words, when we behold (see or observe) the glory of the Lord on the inside, it is reflected on the outside. That true image is displayed when we are out in the open. So next time you go to the store, seek to find the mirror on the other side of the fitting room, because that's the one that will reveal what others will observe.

7

You're Looking into My Heart

In preparation for the Annual Women's Conference in 2015, Pastor Henry, one of the worship leaders, was divinely inspired to sing the words "You're looking into my heart." These words, added to a very powerful worship song, brought a greater realization that God is truly looking into our hearts, inspecting the contents. This brings us to a place of humility. It makes us realize that there is nothing hidden from Him. He knows our thoughts before we can think them.

> *The Lord knows the thoughts of man [and woman], that they are futile.*
>
> —Psalm 94:11

We are compelled and challenged to cultivate pure thoughts towards each other because Christ has pure thoughts about us.

When we read through the book of Psalms, we see that David prayed many prayers as petitions for God to destroy his enemies. But as we examine those prayers, David was sincerely and wholeheartedly praying to God. David did not gather his friends to

> GOD IS TRULY LOOKING INTO OUR HEARTS, INSPECTING THE CONTENTS.

have a bash-my-enemies party. He knew that God had already investigated his heart and knew the contents.

Before David was chosen to be king, all his brothers had to go to Samuel the prophet. In his humanity, Samuel observed the brothers and might have thought, *Well, this one is good-looking; maybe he should be king.* Here is what the Scriptures say about Samuel's selection process:

> *But the Lord said to Samuel, "Do not look at his appearance or at his physical stature, because I have refused him. For the Lord does not see as man sees; for man looks at the outward appearance, but the Lord looks at the heart.*
>
> —1 Samuel 16:7

That powerful declaration—"You're looking into my heart"—still impacts me each time I sing it. He looks into the heart and knows the undiluted measure of His grace that I need. God knows the portion of His love that I need and releases that love into me like an antidote to the soul.

Moses had a great hunger to see and know God for himself. He said to the Lord,

> *And he said, "Please, show me Your glory."*
>
> *Then He said, "I will make all My goodness pass before you, and I will proclaim the name of the Lord before you. I will be gracious to whom I will be gracious, and I will have compassion on whom I will have compassion."*

But He said, "You cannot see My face; for no man shall see Me, and live."

—Exodus 33:18–20

This God, who is so full of glory and greatness, can speak to us individually when we lack confidence. He observes even the garments we select before we head out for our daily activities. He is aware of the miscalculated judgments we place on ourselves. He speaks to that lack, declaring, "I have clothed you in this garment. You don't see yourself the way I see you. It is how I see you."

Regardless of the stipulations of our individual purpose and calling, beyond our personal titles and credentials, before we dress in the morning and set out to accomplish the day's activities, we must remind ourselves that we are clothed in robes of righteousness. We are clothed and sent out as ambassadors. In fact, every gift we bear and every passion we use to define our personalities finds its origin in God. The nature, character, and expression of God has been birthed in each one of us because we are His creation. The Scriptures say, *"Then God said, 'Let Us make man in Our image, according to Our likeness'"* (Genesis 1:26).

When we surrender to His plan for our lives, we come to realize that He is a mission-oriented God. He commissions and sends us out as His representatives and ambassadors. His purpose is to fulfill His promise by demonstrating His love to everyone we interact with. We become carriers of His grace and vessels to transport His love to our neighbours.

In recent months, I have been learning, with a more progressive understanding and heightened vision, about the truths embedded in the Word. One of my greatest desires and aspirations is to know the truth and walk in the full revelation of it.

David, the patriarch, had a similar desire and declared, "*But you desire honesty from the womb, teaching me wisdom even there*" (Psalm 51:6, NLT). My desire to know His truths propels me to examine my life and take inventory of the fruit of the Spirit—identified in Galatians 5:22: love, joy, peace, patience, kindness, goodness, gentleness, and longsuffering (self-control).

If I maintain this fruit in my basket, the Bible tells me that I will have no trouble with the law.

The fruit has multiple characteristics. They describe the attributes of Christ. I endeavour to learn all about these attributes so I can maintain the model, the image and personality of Christ.

When I examine my life, many imperfections still show up. However, they are being chiselled off as I surrender to His care. I know that I am His work in progress, so I aim to keep the fruit intact.

While we give Him permission to work on our imperfections, He extends His grace and favour to us and declares the following over our lives:

- We are free from condemnation (Romans 8:1).
- We are His workmanship and design (Ephesians 2:10).
- We have been reconciled to Christ (Colossians 1:21).
- We have everlasting life (John 5:24).
- Christ is our hope and glory (Colossians 1:27).

- We are a new creation (2 Corinthians 5:17).
- We are declared righteous by God (2 Corinthians 5:21).

Points to Ponder

- In your basket, are the attributes of Christ visible?
- What are your neighbours observing about your fruit?

8

Heart Examination

The Sovereign Lord will go a long way to display His grace to you and me. Time is not an issue and distance is not a hindrance for the release and unveiling of His power in our lives.

The devil knows how to bring temptations to our hearts and minds to derail us and place obstacles in our path. They are often so high that we aren't able to get over them on our first attempt. Nonetheless, we can be assured that there is no temptation that the devil hasn't already used against someone else. It is his plan to detour us, but it is God's plan to advance us.

As followers of Christ, we must be able to discern the evil intents the devil presents before us from time to time.

Not all the situations that occur in our lives are brought on by the devil, though. Sometimes the Lord will permit situations to transpire in our day-to-day lives. Those situations are launched by God so we can perform a thorough examination of our hearts and determine the maturity of our faith.

> *I, the LORD search the heart, I test the mind, even to give every man according to his ways, according to the fruit of his doings.*
>
> —Jeremiah 17:10

9

Stripping Away

A very interesting process seems to happen to me every year. It happens both in the fall and in the spring. It is the shedding of my skin, a process that is so embarrassing. I can't explain why it happens. I don't know when it's going to happen, it just does. It could be my hands and arms, or it could be my feet and legs.

We go through a similar process in our journey with God. We don't know when it's going to happen; we just know that it does. When it happens, we may even metaphorically associate it to a certain season (spring, summer, autumn, winter). We cannot predict how long it is going to last, but we are certain that during the process we will recognize and experience the season. It will be the season in which our personal character is transformed into His predestined design.

What is the duration, you may ask?

Well, that depends on our level of cooperation and obedience.

During the fall season, I passionately observe and admire the transformation of the trees in the backyard. There are many variations of trees. At different intervals during the season, they individually lose their leaves. One particular tree is the last one to lose its leaves in the fall, but it is the first tree to display its worm-like fruit in the spring.

In my observation and admiration, I ask myself some questions. First, if the trees have the knowledge to comprehend their season and operate according to their lifespan, what must my reaction be when I consider the lifespan of a human being? Second, if the branch of a tree comprehends its season and has knowledge and awareness of the day and the hour to send forth its fruit, why do humans question their destiny? Third, why do humans question the destinies of others?

Certainly, there are other questions we seek to clarify. Answers can only come from Him. We have to rest in the confident assurance that we are defined only by Christ. Our identity is found in Him. He has the answers to the questions we seek.

In the Book of Psalms, David prayed,

O Lord, you have examined my heart
and know everything about me.
You know when I sit down or stand up.
You know my thoughts even when I'm far away.
You see me when I travel
and when I rest at home.
You know everything I do.
You know what I am going to say
even before I say it, Lord.
You go before me and follow me.
You place your hand of blessing on my head.
Such knowledge is too wonderful for me,
too great for me to understand!

I can never escape from your Spirit!
I can never get away from your presence!
If I go up to heaven, you are there;
if I go down to the grave, you are there.
If I ride the wings of the morning,
if I dwell by the farthest oceans,
even there your hand will guide me,
and your strength will support me.
I could ask the darkness to hide me
and the light around me to become night—
but even in darkness I cannot hide from you.
To you the night shines as bright as day.
Darkness and light are the same to you.
You made all the delicate, inner parts of my body
and knit me together in my mother's womb.
Thank you for making me so wonderfully complex!
Your workmanship is marvelous—how well I know it.
You watched me as I was being formed in utter seclusion,
as I was woven together in the dark of the womb.
You saw me before I was born.
Every day of my life was recorded in your book.
Every moment was laid out
before a single day had passed.
How precious are your thoughts about me, O God.
They cannot be numbered!
I can't even count them;
they outnumber the grains of sand!

And when I wake up,
you are still with me!...
Search me, O God, and know my heart;
test me and know my anxious thoughts.
Point out anything in me that offends you,
and lead me along the path of everlasting life.
—Psalm 139:1–18, 23–24, NLT

All the questions we may have, whether we seek to find them in the beauty of nature or in the masterpiece of our lives, we can find the answers to our questions in His Word.

Points to Ponder

- Pray and ask God if we are indeed cultivating, producing, and maintaining the fruit He has designed for us to produce.

10

Dew of Heaven

Early one morning I awoke and looked outside to see what appeared to be snow. It was not snow. I had to refocus to see that it was fog. The grass was covered with moisture due to the heavy frost.

It was garbage day, so I went to put the trash out. Thankfully, I didn't have an early-morning appointment that required driving. The fog was so thick that I imagine it would have been difficult to navigate a vehicle through it difficult but not impossible

After dealing with the trash, I sensed a gentle breeze blowing. The fog was being carried along very slowly. I turned in the direction that the fog was traveling, and suddenly felt the particles of fog making contact on my face. I stood for a while looking towards the heavens and experienced the wind and the fog upon my face.

When I returned to the house, my clothes were damp, and my face was wet as though I had been in the rain.

This serves as a reminder of the ways in which the Lord works in our lives. He speaks His purposes to us in a very gentle way. God does not always use the dramatic to communicate His plan and purpose to us. And because there is no drama, we often miss the impact and intent of what He

HE SPEAKS HIS PURPOSES TO US IN A VERY GENTLE WAY.

is saying or what He wants to do. He often uses ordinary means of communication to reveal extraordinary plans. When that happens, there is no question that He is the architect and inventor of those plans. He alone chooses the ways in which He desires to communicate with us.

It's a similar manner in which He spoke to one of the patriarchs, the prophet Elijah, for example:

> *A very powerful wind went before the Lord,* digging *into the mountain and causing landslides, but the Lord was not in the wind. After the windstorm there was an earthquake, but the Lord was not in the earthquake. After the earthquake, there was a fire, but the Lord was not in the fire. After the fire, there was a soft whisper. When Elijah heard it, he covered his face with his robe and went out and stood at the entrance to the cave. All of a sudden a voice asked him, "Why are you here, Elijah?" He answered, "I have been absolutely loyal to the Lord, the sovereign God, even though the Israelites have abandoned the agreement they made with you, torn down your altars, and killed your prophets with the sword. I alone am left and now they want to take my life." The Lord said to him, "Go back the way you came and then head for the Desert of Damascus.*
>
> —1 Kings 19:9–15, NET, emphasis added

Would it not be interesting if we were able to sense and feel the glory of God resting on our bodies, and on our faces, just as the fog descends and rests upon the ground? The fog is dispensed to display its purpose by blanketing the surface with moisture. The fog dissipates when the sun strengthens to shine forth its brilliance. In the same way, when God's glory is displayed through His people, they are empowered to exhibit the brilliance of the Son. We, the people of God, are commissioned to dispense and disseminate His love and grace to accomplish the work that He has sent us to do.

Points to Ponder

- What are your thoughts on the dew of heaven?
- What do you think it feels like?
- If God were to send a windstorm to transport the dew from heaven to earth, would we question why He sends wind and dew at the same time?
- We often sing songs about the dew of heaven and pray that it would rain down upon us. As we seek to get understanding from the heart of the Father of what this means, jot down whatever response He deposits in your heart and spirit.
- Allow Him to release a gentle wind from His throne to saturate you with the dew of heaven. Linger in His presence and be still before Him.

Part II

Merging of Dreams, Visions, and Encounters

Oh Lord, we come now before You.
From the secret place we call.
Our lives, we lay at Your feet and unto You,
We surrender our all.
So here we are in Your presence;
We bow before You and lift up Your name.
Here we are in Your presence;
Oh Lord, You are forever the same.

—Sonia Henry, 1980

11

A Competent Communicator

I am a firm believer that God releases creative ideas and thoughts into our hearts that are designed to capture the sense of His plan and purpose for our lives. I strongly believe that experiences we've had in the past are signposts and markers to identify our destiny. Some experiences are positive and some are very negative. God uses the positive as well as the negative to reveal His truths.

We read the stories of men and women who were positioned for purpose. Today, when we read those accounts, we can say that we have travelled back in time to glean wisdom from their experiences to help propel us forward. Don't dismiss their experiences too quickly; they just may be the catalyst through which the glory of God will be displayed in your life.

Throughout the Scriptures, the Lord spoke to many people. He spoke through and used many different people to demonstrate His power, grace, mercy, and love. We also see in Scripture where animals were used to demonstrate how the majestic God can command their understanding to be subjected to His will and purposes as they surrender to His authority.

Daniel was thrown into the lion's den, but the lion did not destroy him because God spoke to its instinct and removed its inbred nature of destruction. The reality that God can release a measure of understanding into such a creature can overwhelm the mind of the natural man. This particular lion stood as a guardian for the prophet Daniel and protected him from harm and danger (Daniel 6:10–23).

The donkey in Numbers 22 was beaten by Balaam, its master. The Lord awakened the sense of sight in the donkey, and it saw an angel of the Lord standing in the road, preventing it from going forward. When Balaam saw that the donkey knelt down in the road, he began to beat it and thought its stubborn nature was acting up. The conversation between Balaam and donkey, found in Numbers 22, went like this:

> *Then the Lord gave the donkey the ability to speak. "What have I done to you that deserves your beating me three times?" it asked Balaam.*
>
> *"You have made me look like a fool!" Balaam shouted. "If I had a sword with me, I would kill you!"*
>
> *"But I am the same donkey you have ridden all your life," the donkey answered. "Have I ever done anything like this before?"*
>
> *"No," Balaam admitted.*
>
> *Then the Lord opened Balaam's eyes, and he saw the angel of the Lord standing in the roadway with a drawn sword in his hand. Balaam bowed his head and fell face down on the ground before him.*
>
> *"Why did you beat your donkey those three times?" the angel of the Lord demanded. "Look, I have come to block your way because you are stubbornly resisting me.*

> *Three times the donkey saw me and shied away; otherwise, I would certainly have killed you by now and spared the donkey."*
>
> *Then Balaam confessed to the angel of the Lord, "I have sinned. I didn't realize you were standing in the road to block my way. I will return home if you are against my going."*
>
> —Numbers 22:28–34, NLT

Can you imagine the voice of a human emerging from the donkey, directed toward its master? I can just visualize Balaam looking around to see if the other servants who were with him heard him talking to a, well, beast of burden. A donkey was sent forward as a competent communicator and seer, having the ability to view the supernatural.

God commanded a raven to provide bread and meat for the prophet Elijah (1 Kings 17:1–7). Then there was the big fish that demonstrated the gift of hospitality on another level; it was a willing host for Jonah when he was thrown overboard (Jonah 1–2).

Because the sovereign God performed those miraculous deeds through creatures of the wild, He could use humanity to perform miracles that bring glory to His name.

If a beast of burden saw and responded to an angel, if God caused a feathered creature that travelled above the ground and a fish that resided in the sea to submit to His purpose, then certainly He can speak to us and through us for His Kingdom purposes. Men and women, boys and girls, young and old are vessels and instruments for His glory (Joel 2).

In His eyes, no one is of lesser value. We are all equal in His sight. He uses individuals from every nation, tongue, tribe, and people to display His glory. The Scriptures declare that He is the same yesterday, today, and forever (Hebrews 13:8).

We have a lion without an appetite guarding the wellbeing of Daniel.

We have a fish demonstrating impeccable hospitality toward Jonah.

We have a raven trained in the culinary arts to serve Elijah.

We have a donkey, disciplined in the art of communication, speaking to Balaam.

Observe for a moment that these were all prophets. The creatures were used by God to demonstrate a posture of humility in the lives of these prophets.

In the New Testament, we learn of the many gifts that God deposits in the heart and lives of men and women. We read also of the gifts that are often referred to as the "fivefold gifts." The Bible specifically says,

> *And He Himself gave some to be apostles, some prophets, some evangelists, and some pastors and teachers, 12 for the equipping of the saints for the work of ministry, for the edifying of the body of Christ, 13 till we all come to the unity of the faith and of the knowledge of the Son of God, to a perfect man, to the measure of the stature of the fullness of Christ.*
>
> —Ephesians 4:11–13

We see that there was a specific purpose for the giftedness of these individuals who were used as the mouthpiece to deliver the word of God. And we further observe that God used creatures that lack wisdom and understanding to display His authority to gifted prophets. God used these creatures to display humility in the lives of His prophets. We are challenged not only to observe, but to mimic their posture.

Points to Ponder

- What are your special gifts?
- Have you been given a message to deliver and thought you weren't qualified to do it?

12

The Descent of the Bird with the Scroll

I stood in front of the doorway of the barbecue hut outside the main house on my parents' farm. It was around 6:30 p.m. and very quiet. No one was stirring or walking around. Even the animals were silent. I leaned in the left-hand corner of the hut, on the doorpost. When it's that quiet, I would often sit and listen to the birds echoing their last song before nightfall. It was not unusual to sit and admire the doctor birds, crows, hawks, and other exotic feathered creatures that occupy the skyway.

I glanced up at the beautiful blue sky and saw a bird on a descent. Oh, what beauty. It was spectacular. I could not remove my focus from this beautiful bird because it wasn't like the others. As it descended lower and lower, I realized that it was headed in my direction. I straightened my posture in the doorway to have a better view of the gorgeous creature. The bird was white against the perfectly blue sky. Nothing could be compared to the sight.

As the bird came closer, I noticed that there was a cord hanging down, and an even closer view revealed a scroll-like object with the cord wrapped around it. What was this bird doing?

I was captivated by the beauty; I couldn't stand it. And oh, my goodness, it was coming in my direction!

Where is my camera?

Does anyone else see this beauty?

Does this bird have a nest around here on the roof of the barbecue hut?

Have I or the rest of the family missed out on seeing this beauty?

Have they seen this bird before and not said anything about it?

How can it be so white?

I wish I could have taken one of its feathers; they were so perfect.

Oh my goodness, it was coming closer and closer toward me. Was it going to land on my head?

I put my hands on my head for protection.

It was so close to me. I could see its eyes.

It was looking at me.

The scroll in its claw dangled toward me, almost touching my hands.

I was mesmerized. My hands seemed to stick to my head.

"Take it!" I heard from within. The voice sounded like water rolling around inside me

Who said that? I wondered, but I couldn't look around because of the bird—the bird was right here, and if I looked away, I would lose my focus.

"Take it!" the voice said again.

I wasn't able to lift my hands off my head.

Do I take the bird, the scroll, the cord? What do I take?

"Take it!" the voice thundered for the third time.

I managed to lift my right hand and take hold of the cord, all the while looking into the eyes of the beautiful bird. I was shaking, captivated by its beauty.

I felt as though the water-voice that had been thundering inside me was poured out over me. I felt drenched from head to toe.

I continued to fix my gaze on the beauty that had come so close. Then the bird took off, back into the heavens.

My gaze was fixed on its beauty until it passed above and beyond where my natural eyes could focus. I was now able to have a look at what was in my hand, the scroll with the cord around it.

Then I heard the voice again. "That was Me, the Holy Spirit."

I fell on my knees in the doorway of the barbecue hut and immediately glanced upward to see if the bird had returned. No bird, only the voice.

I began to loosen the cord. I did it very cautiously, because I felt wet and didn't want to damage the paper. I unravelled the scroll, and there was a picture of Jesus, with His arms extended as He embraced a group of people. Then I read the words at the bottom of the scroll: "Teach them what I have taught you and I will be with you always. (Matthew 28:20)"

I looked around and found there was no one else around. I suddenly realized that I had just had an encounter with the Lord. I hadn't been physically drenched, but I felt wet on the inside.

> TEACH THEM WHAT I HAVE TAUGHT YOU AND I WILL BE WITH YOU ALWAYS.
> —MATTHEW 28:20

I stood, just in case someone came by and wondered why I was kneeling in the dust. I then realized that the Lord had prepared this time so that nothing and no one would be moving around to distract me. He had orchestrated the entire scene so I could see and hear what He wanted me to see and hear.

That was the vision I experienced at around ten o'clock in the morning on a bright and sunny day. But that was not the end of it. The whole experience unravelled over a period of five days.

13

Cleaning Day

Two days following the vision, it was cleaning day at home. As parents, my husband and I become recipients of so many lovely gifts in the form of special works of art and drawings. My attempts to guard these lovely pieces entailed collecting them in a shoebox. The box was getting full—I was collecting them from my kids' school and Sunday school—and so I decided on Saturday, cleaning day, to discard some of the older pieces. I didn't pay attention to the pieces I had thrown out; I just knew I had kept them long enough, and I needed to make room for more.

Monday was garbage day, and I knew that one of our sons was assigned the chore of emptying the smaller bins from the bedrooms to the larger bins. When Monday morning arrived, my son came in my room, looked into the garbage bin, and decided he wasn't going to empty it. He mumbled something like "Oh, it's not full" and walked away.

I had filled the bin two days earlier. It was full.

When he made the decision to walk away, I'm not sure what happened, but I wasn't able to speak. It felt like a clamp had been placed on my mouth. My tongue was not available to me. You can imagine that as a mother, certainly there was something to be said. But I wasn't able to speak, and he was off to the next room.

God had a plan.

That night, I had a dream. In the dream, I was in conversation with Jesus and we were in a large open field. Some people started to gather around, and as they came He extended His arms around a group of women among them. There were about a dozen women, and He turned to me and said, "Teach them." The scene ended.

When I woke, I was very alert. It was 6:00 a.m. when I glanced at the clock. Immediately, I had the sense to go to my garbage bin, and as I did I began to rummage through the papers I had discarded two days earlier.

What was I looking for exactly? I wasn't certain, but I was convinced that I would know when I saw it.

Sure enough, halfway through my digging, I came across a piece of paper, badly wrinkled—the most crushed-up piece among the discarded works of art.

The paper had a drawing that mimicked what would typically appear in a colouring book. It was a picture of a figure, representing Jesus, with His arms extended to encircle some people—and they resembled a group of women.

Printed at the bottom of this beautiful work of art was the following text: "Teach them what I have taught you and behold, I will be with you to the end of the age (Matthew 28:20)."

The significance of the scroll will be identified in a later section.

14

Joy Robber

It was a special season of my life as I sought to know and experience God in a greater way. I had been teaching a Sunday school class at the time and was questioning whether I should continue teaching or not.

I sought the counsel of the Sunday school superintendent and was encouraged to continue teaching. Even with this confirmation that I was doing what was predestined for me to do, I still had ongoing feelings of inadequacy.

As believers, we are often faced with the challenge of doubt. During these times, we must be fully aware that we recognize the voice of God. The enemy doesn't have any regard for your knowledge of the Word. He will still try to test and tempt you to believe the contrary. Although I had the affirmation of the Sunday school superintendent, as well as a dream from the Lord, I still heard a little whisper in my head with a conflicting message. The Scriptures tell us, *"The thief does not come except to steal, and to kill, and to destroy. I have come that they may have life, and that they may have it more abundantly"* (John 10:10).

It is fully God's intention to recover and restore to His people those things that the devil has stolen, including our joy and confidence in serving the Lord. As I began to walk in the realization that the Lord was with me, I continued to see the words

"Teach them what I have taught you" in several books and other printed material.

One morning as I travelled to work, I saw my bus buddy. I had befriended this woman for about a year, and we looked forward to seeing each other on the bus. We would share our experiences and mutual passion for God's love. She was a member of a Christian book club and regularly received reading materials from a group called the Navigators. She also felt that she had been called to mentor other young women who were fairly new in their faith.

As we conversed this day, my bus buddy retrieved from her bag a book entitled *Reaching Your World: Disciplemaking for Women* by Beth Mainhood.[1] I immediately turned the book over to see the back cover and read the following: "Therefore go and make disciples… teaching them to obey everything I have commanded you (Matthew 28:19–20)." It is evident to me that God was pursuing me to take hold of the plans He had designed for my life. He was speaking loud and clear. I simply needed to surrender and walk on the pathway that He intended.

---

1 Beth Mainhood, *Reaching Your World: Disciplemaking for Women* (Colorado Springs, CO: NavPress, 1986).

15

Provision and Protection

I will praise the Lord at all times.
I will constantly speak his praises.
I will boast only in the Lord;
let all who are helpless take heart.
Come, let us tell of the Lord's greatness;
let us exalt his name together.
I prayed to the Lord, and he answered me.
He freed me from all my fears.
Those who look to him for help will be radiant with joy;
no shadow of shame will darken their faces.
In my desperation I prayed, and the Lord listened;
he saved me from all my troubles.
For the angel of the Lord is a guard;
he surrounds and defends all who fear him.
—Psalm 34:1–7, NLT, emphasis added

My parents were farmers. The survival of the family was dependent on the various fruits and vegetables they planted. The produce they collected from the fields was sold at the market, and I knew when it was market day because Mom and Dad would begin to package all the items in small bundles. They didn't have transportation, so they would often walk to the market. They would leave very early in the morning because they had to walk for about one and a half hours to reach their destination. And they had to arrive early enough to secure a spot for the day.

We lived in the country, so there was no regular taxi service. Some of the wealthier families in the community had a horse or donkey that carried their produce to the market. We didn't have a horse or donkey at that time, but Dad would borrow a donkey when he needed to transport the heavier items.

I recalled being approximately nine years old and gripped by fear. Mom and Dad had told me the night before that they would be off early in the morning, and I had to be in charge of my siblings. At that time, I had two brothers and a sister.

Off they went. It was still very dark outside, and I wasn't able to go back to sleep. My siblings were still sleeping. That was a good thing. It wasn't one of the days that Mom and Dad borrowed the donkey because they had the lightweight produce.

I sat on a chair in one corner of the house as I listened to the sounds of all the crickets and critters as they rustled by. The house wasn't very big. It had two rooms. I shared a room with my siblings, while my parents had the other room.

I was shivering with fear.

Then I heard the sound of hooves entering the backyard. I began to wonder if my parents had borrowed the horse from the neighbour who resided a fifteen-minute walk from our home. (The sounds of the horse were quite distinct from those of the donkey.)

I continued to question why the horse was in the backyard. The neighbour with the horse visited with our family frequently, so the sound of horse hooves on the walkway was familiar. I continued to shiver and shake as another horse arrived. The horses kept coming until there seemed to be ten or twelve of them. I lost count. They encircled the house. My heart was pounding so hard I could barely breathe.

My parents had patches of ornamental grass around the house, and the horses loved to eat it. I could hear the horses pulling and eating the grass. I started to panic. I didn't know how I would explain this to my parents. I would need help with cleaning up all the droppings from the horses. What would I tell them about the grass?

It was nearly an hour since Mom and Dad had left, and it was still dark outside. I was too afraid to lift the curtain and take a peek outside. Maybe the people on the horses would see me if I looked out there and they would come into the house and take us all.

So I sat curled up in the chair, staring at the front door to make sure the bolt remained intact.

My fear eventually subsided, and I no longer shivered with the same intensity. Then finally, I was no longer shivering at all. I mustered up enough courage to peek out the side window, where I could see most of the ornamental grass on the left side of the house.

Daylight had arrived, and my siblings were still sleeping. I was relieved.

There was silence! I no longer heard the horses. I opened the curtain a bit wider, looking for the droppings. Slowly, I opened the front door and looked outside. I looked to the left and the right. There was nothing. Nothing was disturbed. There were no droppings. There were no horses. All the grass was still there.

Then what were those sounds? I wondered.

I went through the whole day double-checking everything to ensure the horses hadn't destroyed anything around the yard. It turned out that nothing was discovered and nothing was said.

Young children have experiences and encounters that require as much recognition as the experiences of adults. God desires to speak to and through them with equal authority. As adults, we sometimes repeat the statement "We are born with a purpose." I strongly believe that if we say those things, we should also believe them.

My age was not a factor when I had the encounter with the horses. My parents had trusted me to manage my siblings for the entire day. The natural instinct of a child would be to tell his or her parents the full story, in detail, of what happened after they left during the scary dark hours of the night. I chose to keep the whole thing to myself. Until the writing of this book, no one has heard the whole intense story.

He dispatched His guards to "encamp" around us and protect us.

For year after year, I kept asking the Lord what that experience meant. I've even asked if it was a figment of my imagination. I am confident that it was not. It was a factual experience. Then one day, not very long ago, the Lord showed me that a seed of fear had been planted in me, even as a young child, and He dispatched His guards to "encamp" around us and protect us.

My parents were always praying. They gathered us as children on a regular basis and prayed for God's protection and provision. I believe my experience was a response from God to their petition. They had no knowledge that the response to their petition came in such a tangible way. I never told them what happened.

As I reflect back, I know my parents would have been overjoyed to hear about the encounter and how the Lord protected their children during their absence.

16

Responding Worshipfully

My mother passed away, and I had just returned from her funeral. One month went by before I learned about the death of another family member, a cousin. I felt compelled to pay my respects by attending the funeral service. The drive was about four hours from home. My beloved and I arrived at the church for the service.

The memories of my mother's funeral came rushing into my mind and began to overwhelm me. I guess it was evident that I was still a bit sensitive and still in mourning. I came in contact with several individuals who expressed their condolences in memory of my mother, and as well I met others who, though they were aware of her passing, chose to say nothing. Emotions are usually a bit fraught during those times. When we become believers and followers of Jesus Christ, it doesn't mean we have to put our emotions on hold. Jesus displayed His emotions; when He came to the burial place of Lazarus, He wept.

The two sisters of Lazarus—Mary and Martha—demonstrated their anxious emotional state (John 11:1–44). We often experience limited vocabulary when someone we love is grieving. The things we say to the grieving individual must be carefully wrapped in grace, love, and peace.

Our faith to believe the promises of God is only activated within the timeframe that He has predestined. The plan might appear to be very close, but until the clock strikes the hour, it is not fully the time. The promises He makes are worth the wait. Martha ran to see Jesus outside of the place where He intended to display the glory of God. As a result, we see that she wasn't able to fully grasp the idea that it was God's intention to raise Lazarus from the dead. When we attempt to operate outside of the boundaries of time and purpose, we experience doubt and disappointment.

Sometimes we have a situation in our lives that we are unable to control. We may feel that God is taking His time responding to our prayer, and the issue appears to be out of control. Rest assured, He is never late. We have His promise from Hebrews 13:5: *"I will never leave you nor forsake you."* Jesus Himself has declared that promise, and it is impossible for Him to go back on His word. When Lazarus died, Jesus was not delayed because He was tied up in a traffic jam. He took His time so that the faith of Mary and Martha could be activated to ensure the Father would get the glory.

Let us encourage ourselves and not give up if we have poor health, if we don't get our dream job, or if we don't easily recognize our own gifts and talents.

While you wait to receive the answer, worship.

While Martha waited… well, she was still in the kitchen, and she was angry. I think Martha had a bit of jealousy toward Mary. She knew that Jesus loved her just as much as He loved Mary, but she sought affirmation and admiration based on the things she did rather than seeking the affection of Christ and passionately worshiping Him. Cooking and cleaning—the hospitality stuff—is what Martha did best.

As soon as Martha found out that Jesus had arrived, she hurried out to meet Him and said, *"Lord, if You had been here, my brother would not have died"* (John 11:21). In her grief, she somehow lost her focus. Her statement had an accusatory tone. She wasn't able to comprehend that Jesus was the resurrection and the life (John 11:25).

Sometimes the Lord speaks to us, but we are so busy filtering our day-to-day clutter that we don't hear Him clearly. We have to develop the skill of listening between the lines. That is, we not only listen with our natural ears; we listen and hear with our supernatural ears.

There are times when we may not be aware that we are being audited (being checked upon when we're not looking). The auditors could be in our workplaces, in our families, in the church, or even in the doctor's office. I recall one doctor who told me that he deliberately delayed my going in to see him during my scheduled appointment because he wanted to see the results of my blood pressure after I had gone through the stress of waiting. It was fine when he measured it, but my blood pressure became elevated after he told me that.

So Mary was being checked out. Those who came to sit in the social gathering and pay their respects and offer their condolences to the family—they observed how she calmly waited for Jesus to arrive. As soon as Mary learned of Jesus' arrival, she ran out of the house and those who had been sitting with her ran after her to continue their audit. As soon as she saw Jesus, *"she fell down at His feet, saying to Him, 'Lord, if You had been here, my brother would not have died'"* (John 11:32).

Are we able to come to that point of believing that He can take our pain? Or do we give ourselves permission to say things without filtering them through His grace or through the knowledge that He is the "I am"? Mary said the same thing to Jesus as Martha did. The difference is that Martha's comment was filtered through her inability to believe. Because she didn't believe, her desire to understand what Jesus was telling her about Himself didn't register. Mary's statement, although the exact same as her sister's, had a different tone. Her comments were filtered through a heart of worship toward her Lord.

From reading this story, we glean that Jesus often visited the home of Lazarus, Mary, and Martha. He was a family friend. Due to the regular visits, there was an expectation that Martha should have known more about Jesus. Their friendship was based primarily on the social dynamics that prevailed as they interacted in their community. Mary was a habitual worshipper. Whether it was in her family room or on the main artery of the town of Bethany—Scripture does not say where Jesus met them that day—she responded to Him worshipfully.

Jesus wants to speak life into the situations we encounter. He wants to unravel the bandages so we can emerge from our places of confinement and walk in freedom. Equally important, He has positioned others beside us to assist with the unravelling and unveiling. His purposes for our lives are carried out in partnership with Himself and the Holy Spirit. Ultimately, it is for His glory.

Jesus wanted to unravel the bandages wrapped from head to toe in the midst of the mourning process I was going through. He wanted to unwrap the emotional state I was trapped in.

One week after attending my cousin's funeral, I was expected to travel to the U.S. for an annual women's conference. To be honest, I didn't feel up to it because I still felt depressed. Sometimes we just have to encourage ourselves, leave the sad feelings behind, and press forward toward the goal of obtaining the prize of a higher calling in Christ Jesus (Philippians 3:14).

My beloved and I both travelled to the conference (there was a segment set aside for the men who attended). So, bright and early on Saturday morning, he was off to his men's breakfast meeting. I headed to the breakfast lounge where I met some of the other ladies who had also travelled to the conference. We were a group of eight sitting at a round table. We fellowshipped and discussed the events of the evening before.

When breakfast was done, I felt the urge to purchase a book from the hundreds of books that were available. The others remained seated, and I excused myself.

Before I left the table, I glanced toward the door and noticed a very tall lady standing in the doorway. As I looked at her, our eyes met and she began to walk towards my table.

"Are you leaving?" she asked.

"Yes," I responded. "You're welcome to have my seat."

"Will you be coming back?"

"No, I'm planning to go back to my room to do some reading."

Then I left. All the while, I had this nagging feeling in my stomach that I needed to go back to the breakfast table.

Immediately after purchasing my books, I returned to the table.

The tall lady was *still* looking at me.

As I sat down she said, "I'm glad you came back to the table, because I have a song for you!"

I thought, *Who is this lady and why does she think I want to hear a song?*

"Yes, I have a song for you," she repeated.

I thought that perhaps I had said something out loud and she'd heard the hesitation in my voice.

"What is your song and why do you want to sing it for me?" I asked.

She stood up, came around to the other side of table, sat in the vacant seat beside me, and began to sing these words:

Be who I've made you to be.
Take My hand and come walk with Me.
Your future is bright can't you see,
If you come and dine with Me.

Reach who I need you to reach
And teach those who I sent you to teach.
Reach out and touch and pour out My love.
You are not on your own; you have the Heavenly Dove.

You may not know who you are,
But as you look to Me, I am bringing you far.
Shake off the past and the pain;
They only pull you back like a rein.

Walk with Me.
I will set you free.
I'll bring you perfect peace.
Take My hand.
Choose to stand.
I'm bringing you into your land.

Do not be anxious or strive
And do not think that you've arrived.
It is My Spirit in you that makes you thrive.
If you are stuck in a place where you are seeking My face,
Then you'll be who I've made you to be.

There is nothing on earth that will satisfy like being who you are; you are a star.
You have been made one of a kind.
You are the head, not the tail.
You are the front, not behind.
And one more thing: remind yourself to sing a joyful song.

Be who I made you to be.
By my death, I have set you free.
And you know that forgiveness is the key.

Receive my forgiveness and set yourself free.
Release all of those who you have had aught against. And you will proceed.
Come out from behind the fence,
To be who I have made you and called and anointed you to be
Who I've made you to be.

By the time this song was over, I was an absolute mess—tears everywhere. Initially, I saw the individual as a very tall lady. God can do anything He wants to demonstrate His glory, love, and grace. Perhaps the tall lady had been at the conference since the previous day. I don't know. What I do know is that it was impossible to miss her because of her height.

> THERE IS NOTHING ON EARTH THAT WILL SATISFY LIKE BEING WHO YOU ARE; YOU ARE A STAR.

It became evident that God transformed her so that, in my eyes, she took on the appearance of an angel. I only recognized the angelic characteristics after she had completed the song she had been sent to sing.

Remember the story of the donkey? Balaam hadn't recognized the angel who stood in the road. After the donkey kneeled down and refused to budge, God opened Balaam's eyes and he saw the angel.

The tall lady was an angel of the Lord, and He had sent her to that breakfast hall to minister His peace to my heart and mind. I was hurting. I didn't walk around telling people that I was hurting, but God knew I was hurting and He was looking into my heart. He saw my anguish over the loss of my mother. God opened my eyes to see that He had sent an angel to sing a song that symbolized the healing oil that is poured out on a wound. He is a very gentle God, and He does powerful things.

You may be wondering how I got the words of the song. Well, one of the ladies at the table had a recording gadget. She recorded and transcribed the song for me.

17

A Fragrant Encounter

Early one morning, I went out for my daily stroll. It was a part of my morning routine before going to work. I scheduled twenty minutes to reach my destination and twenty minutes to get back.

Ten minutes after starting out, I arrived at a spot with dense trees. Along the side of the road was a walking bicycle path and a conservation site.

I chose to walk on the roadway, as a safety precaution. The area was not completely developed and there were still some vacant lots slated for future development.

Suddenly, I detected a fragrance. It was the most beautiful fragrance I have ever experienced.

I kept walking.

After about ten steps, the scent faded, and I thought, *I would love to find the flower or plant that released such a beautiful fragrance. It would make a good conversation piece for visitors to my garden.*

I made my way back, ten steps. I started to sniff around the area, but the fragrance was no longer there.

It was the beginning of spring and we still had snow on the ground; there were no buds on the trees yet. I looked thoroughly in the bushes to see if I could locate the plant. Nothing was growing out from under the snow.

At that moment, I knew it was the presence of the Lord. I was unable to continue my morning stroll. I chose instead to rest in the thought that I had just experienced the presence of the Lord dispensed in a fragrant aroma.

Later that day, I read a poetic rendition of beauty and love found in the Song of Solomon:

Look, the winter is past,
and the rains are over and gone.
The flowers are springing up,
the season of singing birds[a] has come,
and the cooing of turtledoves fills the air.
The fig trees are forming young fruit,
and the fragrant grapevines are blossoming.
Rise up, my darling!
Come away with me, my fair one!

—Song of Solomon 2:11–13, NLT.

18

Activating Faith

We lived in Montreal before moving to Ottawa. Transitions are not always a calm phase of life, but when we are empowered and armed with God's strength we can transition in His strength.

In the years leading up to our transition to Ottawa, God began to show us some amazing things. Even then, we knew He was working in our lives but didn't know how it would turn out in the end. He was speaking to my heart and, at the same time, uncovering His truths to one of my colleagues, Jessi.

Jessi was experiencing layers of relationship issues, and it was evidently interfering with her work. Under the umbrella of Billy Graham, there was a crusade planned in Montreal, and I thought this would be my opportunity to encourage her. Although I felt promptings to tell her the truth and provide her with solutions, I thought it would be best for someone with more experience to tell her that Jesus was the answer to the issues she was experiencing. You see, this is one of the ways we try to get out of doing what we have been called to do. When we do that, we are only delaying our destiny.

One morning shortly after arriving at work, I approached Jessi and asked if she had heard of Billy Graham.

"Oh yes," she said. "He's that guy on TV who's always talking about God."

Well, this was my cue to invite her, so I did and she accepted my invitation. My heart rejoiced when she said yes.

We went to the meeting as we had planned. I had received the training and was set to be on duty that evening as one of the prayer councillors.

Jessi selected her seat. I wanted to sit with her, but I could sense that something incredible was going to take place with her.

Once the event was in progress, I went to sit with her for a while. I excused myself halfway through the session because I observed that she was engaged in what was happening. I didn't want our friendship to get in the way of what God wanted to do with her.

This hockey arena was big, with a seating capacity of twenty thousand. I sat down about two rows back from Jessi, where she could see me if she had a question or simply needed some reassurance.

Soon it was time for the altar call. The mass of people began to go forward, including those sitting on the other side of her. I was praying hard, really hard, that Jessi would go forward. She did not. However, the Spirit of God descended upon her right there, and she began to shake so hard that she was almost bouncing up and down in her seat. I was glad that the seats around her were vacant, because there was sure to have been some collision with her neighbours had they still been seated beside her.

Tears began to flow from her eyes. I still didn't approach her. She had an encounter, and I wanted her to come away from the crusade knowing that she'd had the experience of a lifetime.

Those who went forward received some material and an information kit for follow-up and further guidance. Before the meeting, the councillors were provided with packages of the handouts, so I was able to provide Jessi with a package before we left.

On our way home, she was very quiet. I was doing the talking, and no matter what I asked her, she only answered say yes or no. Before we parted, I said a simple prayer with her that God would protect her and protect what He had deposited in her. We both went home knowing that we would see each other at work the following day.

Thursday arrived, and we met in the office. Jessi quietly informed me that she hadn't slept the night before, yet she looked completely rested. There was a remarkable glow to her countenance.

I asked if she recalled her experience from the day before. She said she had felt someone lifting her up and placing her on a pedestal, and she felt as though she was still sitting there.

The days, weeks, and months went by, and Jessi's life completely changed. The relational issues she had been experiencing disappeared. A shakeup happened at that arena, and it took a while for everything to settle down. I had the opportunity to walk through her experiences with her and share some of the truths that reside in the word of God.

One way to identify the truth is to demonstrate how faith works. Two years before we moved to Ottawa, God spoke to my heart and said, "I will relocate your family to Ottawa where you will be ministers in My churches." Naturally, when something like that comes into your mind, the normal reaction is to dismiss it.

God doesn't want to change things right now, I thought.

I pondered those words in my heart and didn't repeat them to anyone, not even to my beloved. I prayed about it continuously.

On another day, probably about two weeks later, I felt God give me a timeframe in which this word would come to pass. "It will be in two years," I heard Him say when I presented my question to Him in prayer.

Armed with a deadline, I thought, *I'm going to exercise my faith. I want to prove God in this area.* I reminded myself of what the Scriptures say: *"Now faith is the substance of things hoped for, the evidence of things not seen"* (Hebrews 11:1). I armed myself with the confidence that I knew God had spoken to me.

I confided in Jessi and asked her not to share the information with anyone else. I shared with her that in two years, I would be making an announcement to relocate our family to Ottawa. She looked at me with wide eyes. I reassured her that when I made the announcement, she would have solid proof of what happens when we have faith in God.

"Okay, let's go to the door," Jessi said, joking around. "I want to see which one of us gets out of this office first."

We both stood in the doorway attempting to see who would get out first. It was hilarious. None of us succeeded.

We left it at that and concluded that if God had spoken this word, He was going to bring it to pass.

Nearly one year had passed when, on the way to our Sunday morning worship meeting, my beloved piped up and said, "I have been feeling in my spirit that God is calling us to move to Ottawa, and our mandate will be to minister to the leaders of different churches."

I nearly fell out of the car.

As I managed to contain myself, my first question was, "How long have you known this?"

"Just over a year," he replied.

Only at that time did I release to my beloved that God had spoken to my heart about the same thing, almost the exact words, just over a year ago. I also disclosed to him that I had shared it with Jessi as a way of encouraging her in her newfound faith.

The first thing we did was celebrate the goodness of God by giving Him praise that He had communicated this thought to both of us at the same time, although independently. The next thing we did was pray that He would continue to pour His revelation into our hearts about what to do next.

God is in the business of aligning His people for His purposes and plans for their lives.

19

Sitting in the Doorway

Sitting or standing in a doorway signifies many different things, to my understanding. One, a doorway represents a place of need where a person desires for something more but has a hesitation or reluctance to go through the door to obtain it. Two, it signifies a place of shame and embarrassment. Something may have happened behind those doors to inhibit the freedom of entry through that doorway again. Third, it represents a place of maturity in the foundations of faith.

God requires that while we are sitting (or standing) in a doorway, we pray, waiting and listening for His call. He will open doors that no man can shut and shut doors that no man can open (Revelation 3:7–8). When we position ourselves in the doorway of His purposes, we will not be able to go in or out until that which He has purposed comes into alignment with His will.

A beautiful story develops in 2 Kings about a wealthy woman (often referred to as the Shunammite woman) and her husband who were socially prominent and regularly provided a place for Elisha the prophet to stay. Because of the frequency of Elisha's visits, they decided to build a room in their home to accommodate him. Elisha thought of repaying her for the kindness she demonstrated, but he was unaware of her needs. Elisha, through his servant, asked what he could do to repay her kind concern and hospitality. She initially stated that she had no need. Then, Elisha's servant investigated:

> *Later Elisha asked Gehazi, "What can we do for her?"*
>
> *Gehazi replied, "She doesn't have a son, and her husband is an old man."*
>
> *"Call her back again," Elisha told him. When the woman returned, Elisha said to her as she stood in the doorway, "Next year at this time you will be holding a son in your arms!"*
>
> *"No, my lord!" she cried. "O man of God, don't deceive me and get my hopes up like that."*
>
> *But sure enough, the woman soon became pregnant. And at that time the following year she had a son, just as Elisha had said.*
>
> —2 Kings 4:14–17, NLT

Remember Jessi and me in the doorway? Neither of us were able to get out. We weren't able to get out because that symbolic act demonstrated that her faith had not yet aligned with God's purpose. In other terms, there was no purpose to attempting to get out the door. What Jessi needed was to experience the fulfillment of the word I had shared with her and understand the workings of faith at that point in her development.

At the same time, God was aligning His plan in both my beloved and me. He knew the season and time when we would become unified in our mindsets as to take the next step that was our destiny in Him. We could not engage in a process which we had not been released to do.

So we continued to wait. God was setting everything up for our transition to Ottawa. Looking back, it was an incredible period of preparation. Many different individuals were involved in the process. And while they were involved, they were not fully aware of what was going on.

> *And we know that all things work together for good to those who love God, to those who are the called according to His purpose.*
>
> —Romans 8:28

20

A Declaration of Hope

There is a shift that is coming to the earth.
I can feel it in my spirit. I see God standing at the threshold to the nations of this world. He is waiting with the sceptre of grace and judgment in His hand.
He is standing at the threshold and He is ready to showcase His righteousness. He is lining up, and He is positioning His guards at the doorways; they stand at the at the entrance ways. As He extends His sceptre,
He declares, "These are called
My House of Hope."
There will be no banner to announce the places. The Spirit and the Authority of God will reveal and release the knowledge and the understanding to His people as they walk by the Houses.

21

The Deception

Deception is not the way the Father wants to lead His children.

I wasn't able to sleep one night. I lay awake as my mind began to complete some projects. I was planning the ingredients for the next meal (that would be supper, since my beloved took care of breakfast).

Suddenly, I had a vision. I saw a light come into the room—and then a human form appeared. I was very still, but the figure saw me as we exchanged a glance.

The figure wore a white garment with long and very wide sleeves. The garment had a black belt tied at the front. I then recognized that she was female. She would not maintain her gaze; she kept looking downwards.

The light that had preceded still shone, and I was able once again to make full eye contact with her. She stood at the foot of the bed. Her eyes filled with tears. She simply wasn't able to maintain her focus, so she lowered her head toward the floor again. I sensed that she wanted to say something. She looked downwards with a continuous flow of tears. The light that had come with her began to diminish until gradually there was no light at all. I glanced toward the window in the direction where the light had initially appeared.

I immediately returned my gaze. And when I did, in that split second, she was no longer there.

That was weird, I thought.

Before I could complete my thought, before I could go into the process of analyzing what had just happened, I heard the Lord's voice say, "That was a deception."

Through prayer and meditation on scripture, I learned that the enemy presents and disguises himself and masquerades as an angel of light. 2 Corinthians 11:14–15 says,

> *And no wonder! For Satan himself transforms himself into an angel of light. Therefore it is no great thing if his ministers also transform themselves into ministers of righteousness, whose end will be according to their works.*

22

Discerning and Disarming Deceptions

The visit I received, through the vision, was a definite attempt from one of Satan's ministers to bring a measure of confusion to my tired mind—to destroy my mind. He dispatched one of his ministers to show up in a deceptive light because he thought I was asleep and would not be alert. The enemy knows some things about us, but he doesn't know everything, and we shouldn't give him permission to know anything about us. He should know that we, as God's children, are armed and dangerous.

From personal experience, I've observed that when someone is not telling the truth, they will have difficulty looking you in the eye—and if they do, it will only last for about a second.

Thieves operate in the environment of deception. They target places where there is no light. Their preference is to operate in the dark. If the thief accidentally discovers someone, their goal is to injure or destroy that person.

The Scriptures tell us,

> *The thief does not come except to steal, and to kill, and to destroy. I [Jesus] have come that they may have life, and that they may have it more abundantly.*
>
> —John 10:10

The motive of the enemy is the same as the thief who breaks in when no one is home.

As followers of Christ, we must pattern our thoughts and minds after the mind of Christ so we may discern and disarm the deceptions of the enemy.

We are called to be children of light (1 Thessalonians 5:5). We must safeguard and protect the investment that has been given to us by God—that is, His magnificent love, peace, and protection. Let's not allow ourselves to be burglarized or charmed by a light that offers only temporary illumination.

Points to Ponder

- In the light of God, do we recognize the glow of deception?

Part III

Running the Race

But those who wait on the Lord will find new
strength.
They will soar high on wings like eagles.
They will run and not grow weary.
They will walk and not faint.

—Isaiah 40:31, NLT

23

What's in that Room?

There were days and even nights when I felt like I wanted to run with all my might. I wanted to run away because I knew I would receive a visit; someone was bound to show up—perhaps unexpectedly. I wasn't prepared for the visit because I had some "stuff" hidden away and I didn't want it to be discovered, and I didn't want to provide an explanation.

Sometimes parents would drop in without prior notice, and the house was not always in proper order. Certainly the parents were welcome to come, but I wished they would have called ahead. I didn't want them to see that I just started to sweep the house, and the dust pile was still in the middle of the hallway. I didn't want them to see that I'd had to leave the dust pile there because the washing machine had been overflowing with bubbles. I'd simply dumped too much detergent in the washer. I'd forgotten that the pot was on the stove. I'd been cooking the last six pieces of chicken drumsticks I had pulled from the freezer.

The doorbell rang and immediately Mom and Dad walked in.

Mom asked the loaded question: "Oh honey, what's burning?"

I knew she would go on about my cooking. It never failed; my cooking was not as good as hers.

I prepared myself to get the usual lecture. It went like this: "You didn't spend enough time in the kitchen to learn the secrets about *not* burning the food."

By the time she was done lecturing, I was already in the other room with wads of cotton in my ears. I didn't want a cooking lesson. I think Mom got the message—at least for today.

My husband was expected home any minute, but I still didn't get the chance to hide the six new pairs of shoes with matching handbags under the bed. I know he was going to ask the dreaded question: "Shopping again? Did you buy more shoes and purses?"

I would just wait until he opened the closet in the other room to discover the four new dresses I'd bought—on sale, of course. The original tag was still showing on the labels.

With my mother's lectures and my husband's questions, yes, I wanted to run. Let's not go there!

24

A Reason to Run

I ran away from many situations. It was a coping mechanism I'd learned in my childhood. I had to get away from any situation that made me feel uncomfortable. I might still have some residue of the undesirable situations that left scar tissue. Jesus is the one who can resurface and remove all evidence of scars.

I'm the first one to admit that I'm a work in progress. Until Jesus declares me perfect, I am not perfect.

So in recognition that I have been destined to run a different race, I arrive at this juncture. I am at a crossroads in the plan of God.

It became evident as I arrived at this crossroads that my life was like a house about to have a visitor. Here comes Jesus. He made the announcement in my spirit. He declared that all the closets and rooms would be audited.

Some things were out of alignment and needed to be adjusted. These are the sorts of things that only fathers know how to fix. They just seem to have the right tool for the right project. It's no different with our Heavenly Father. He knows how things work and knows how to fix them even when there are no apparent solutions. When situations become fragmented and dismantled, we make some meagre attempt at locating the tools to reconnect the dangling pieces. Our Heavenly Father is ready to guide and assist.

I was enrolled in part-time studies for nearly ten years. At the beginning of the final semester, I had to complete a "request to graduate" form within a certain timeframe. Following the submission, I made the declaration of my intention to graduate. When I made the announcement, I had no idea what was about to take place. I had been feeling that things couldn't continue as they had been for almost ten years.

It would appear that the Lord had been preparing a position for my beloved to transition into another area of specialization, in the same line of work. He'd desired a change for many years but never applied for it. I can see now that God had held just such a job for him, and it was released at the right time. He still didn't apply for it. Instead the opportunity was presented to him, and he didn't refuse it.

During the same period, the management in my office had evolved—everyone did what was right in his or her own eyes. With much prayer and fasting, three months later, I felt it necessary to take a leave of absence.

During this period of leave, the Lord began to identify some areas that had gone into disrepair and needed renovation—the rooms I spoke about earlier—and the time had come.

On a popular home renovation television show, homeowners seek out a professional with the capacity to transform different rooms in their homes. When the room (or rooms) have been identified, the expert poses these questions: "Are you willing to hand over the keys and trust me in your home? Do you authorize me to make the decision about the cost?" With that agreement, the homeowners must surrender the keys and be willing to leave their home for the period it takes to complete the renovation.

The expert makes the decisions as to the timeframe of the renovation, which room will most benefit from the renovation, and how much it will cost to complete the task. At the end, when the owners are invited back into their home, they are so taken up by the transformation and beauty that the cost becomes secondary.

I've done the math and calculated that the Lord had it all planned for me. I had to take the leave to complete the renovation, repairs, and realignment. Not only that, I needed to rekindle the passion I had for the things of God and the intimacy I once knew. I had developed habits over the years while I was studying, and I had converted those habits into excuses. I'd had many papers to write and didn't have as much time to spend in the Word.

Now you know the reason I wanted to run—not only from the physical house, but also from the spiritual.

25

The Selection of Candidates

I grew up in the Caribbean countryside where we had lots of mountains. In fact, my parents lived between three separate mountains with refreshing spring water flowing down each of them. For the purpose of survival, we had the opportunity to go up and down any of those mountainsides to get water. That was an awesome privilege. We drew water from a never-ending spring—for drinking, cooking, cleaning, bathing, and feeding the animals. So we took many trips up and down the mountainsides on a daily basis.

The opportunity came for some members of my family to emigrate from Jamaica to Canada when I was in my tween years. When I later visited my family in Jamaica, my mother reminded me that I used to run everywhere there.

I asked her if she recalled why I wanted to run everywhere.

"You were afraid of the thunder," Mother said. She also told me that when she wanted something from the shops, and there was rain in the forecast, she would ask me to go. "I knew you would go and return quickly."

I told my mother that it had been an unfair trick.

The selection process for a running candidate is very specific. The individual must recognize his or her potential and ability to run. With care and determination, the coach takes on the responsibility to have the individual tested, and following the results, the coach makes a final judgment to affirm the individual as a runner. He or she is acknowledged as an athlete. The athlete's ability is then measured by rigorous training to determine the particular activity that is the best fit for them. After that, the training becomes more targeted.

It was a surprise to me when my school's physical education teacher selected me. I had not been seeking to do that. He based his selection on what he had observed during my performance in the regular gym classes. He had noticed the scores on my performance chart and came to see me.

That is such a perfect image of God. The plans He has mapped out for us will go forward no matter what. We don't need to ask for Him to give them to us. He does, however, require that we remain obedient, be a willing participant in whatever He is doing, and maintain a teachable heart.

Years after competing in several events and competing in and out of town, I was selected to run in the 4 x 100 relay for the Montreal Olympics of 1976. I was selected to carry the torch for one kilometre and then transfer it to another runner. This opportunity didn't materialize, however, because I wasn't approved. At that time, I experienced multiple levels of disappointment. These disappointments lasted for many years. I've learned, only recently, that I wasn't released by God to run in those races. I had been selected and trained to run a different race.

At the outset of writing this book, I received a call from my sister to see how I was doing. She is not my sibling, but we are such good friends that I refer to her as my sister. We've known each other for many years and she is familiar with my story. I confided in her regarding the writing project I was about to engage in. We encouraged each other, prayed, and said our goodbyes until next time. About two weeks later, I received a note of encouragement from her in the mail. She wrote,

> *He did not want you to "run" for a temporal, worldly prize and, as you realize now, it was His plan for you to "run" a much more important "race." This "race" has an eternal crown, and will affect the lives of many. It may take even more stamina and endurance than any Olympic competition, but it has a much greater prize. By His grace, His power, His strength, His endurance you will "run" and you will have grace and much blessing.*

26

Run with Excellence

We cannot have excess baggage or clothing if we want to win the race. The extra stuff will hold us back. All the hours spent on training will be lost if we continue to wear or carry extra weight. There are instances when we run not because we want to compete but merely because we want to maintain a certain level of fitness, for health reasons. For whatever reason you or I take on the challenge to run, we must run with excellence and freedom.

This kind of running doesn't match the characteristics of the *different* race I had to run. I attempted to run away from some of the situations I was unable to triumph over. Only when I made the decision to participate in the race He has called me to run did I begin to gain victory over the hurdles that once blocked my path. Those hurdles were major hindrances on the pathway toward the prize.

While I was training, I focused on short distances; I was a sprinter and not a long-distance runner. The disciplinary training and encouragement I received from the coach were necessary to build my character and athleticism. It was also the preparation I required to compete as an athlete with full confidence and endurance.

Entering into a race is like entering a battle. The athletes have to be armed with multiple abilities and be flexible to fill the gap in other events when necessary.

The promise of obtaining the prize is hinged on God's plan of gaining the victory and completing the race. To the Hebrews, Paul wrote,

> *Therefore, since we are surrounded by such a huge crowd of witnesses to the life of faith, let us strip off every weight that slows us down, especially the sin that so easily trips us up. And let us run with endurance the race God has set before us. We do this by keeping our eyes on Jesus, the champion who initiates and perfects our faith. Because of the joy awaiting him, he endured the cross, disregarding its shame. Now he is seated in the place of honor beside God's throne.*
>
> —Hebrews 12:1–3, NLT

So why did I run? I ran for the joy of winning the race and obtaining the prize. I wanted to satisfy my fleshly desire through the power of competition.

> THE PROMISE OF OBTAINING THE PRIZE IS HINGED ON GOD'S PLAN OF GAINING THE VICTORY AND COMPLETING THE RACE.

As we begin this journey, we will appreciate that Jesus is calling us to take a parallel route—the one travelled by Paul the Apostle—to complete the race and reach the end of Paul's journey. We will even note some of the principles Paul adhered to so he could claim his prize.

The journey compares to fighting a battle. Paul reminds us that when we engage in battle, we must remain strong and be aware that

> *we do not wrestle against flesh and blood, but against principalities, against powers, against the rulers of the darkness of this age, against spiritual hosts of wickedness in the heavenly places.*
>
> —Ephesians 6:12

> *We have to stand our ground with the authority and knowledge we've gained from our practice and disciplinary sessions. The race is all about our ability to finish with full strength. It is a test of endurance. Go for the gold; it is the top prize. Again, Paul said,* "I press toward the goal for the prize of the upward call of God in Christ Jesus."
>
> —Philippians 3:14

27

The Discipline

Running the 800-metre was, for me, like running long distance. The distance is two times around the standard track. Running that event at full speed was enough to make me pass out. In fact, I did pass out a few times. Runners were often required to complete the 800-metre in the full noonday sun. Thankfully, that was not a regular occurrence for me.

The coach was a wonderful motivator and encourager. The discipline was painful and the consistent hours of training rigorous. I recall having to do the same activity over and over until the timing was perfect to the coach's satisfaction. Between the practice runs, we didn't have much time for rest and recovery. The intense training would only pay off on competition day.

The coach's intention was to ensure that he instructed us in the techniques that would build both our mental and physical strength and develop proper flexibility and agility. He often corrected my flaws as well as the flaws of other team members so we did not repeat our errors.

> "THE QUALITY OF YOUR PREPARATION DETERMINES THE QUALITY OF YOUR PERFORMANCE."

In his handbook titled *Scriptures Every Achiever Should Memorize,* author Mike Murdock wrote,

"The quality of your preparation determines the quality of your performance."[2] This is vital knowledge.

It was very easy to become discouraged. I even entertained thoughts of quitting. Those were the times when the coach's voice echoed louder than normal. His command to get moving would challenge me to get out of my slump. I had to constantly remind myself why I was running: the coach called for me to run, and I enjoyed it. I had to invoke positive thoughts, even when my muscles ached and I didn't feel like I would make it.

Paul experienced many moments of discouragement, and perhaps he, too, wanted to quit. But he was always conscious that he was called to run a race, and he was determined to be an overcomer and a winner. He was motivated to live by faith, to walk in love, and to have hope, particularly in the fact that he expected a prize at the end of the race.

Paul had learned to push ahead. He knew that the secret of discipline resides in having confidence in the Lord. Discipline is an essential factor for everyone who desires to walk in spiritual maturity. He modelled this for others to ensure that they would also confidently complete their race. Paul said, "*And also if anyone competes in athletics, he is not crowned unless he competes according to the rules*" (2 Timothy 2:5).

---

2 Mike Murdock, *Scriptures Every Achiever Should Memorize* (Fort Worth, TX: The Wisdom Centre, 2003), 2.

28

Never Give Up

Some athletes discontinue training before they reach their goal. There are several reasons why they stop. One is that they aren't able to endure the rigorous training and the hours required. When the athlete is ready, he or she will have discovered that it's an investment, and they have to make the proper contribution. The proper contribution will offer beneficial and rewarding results.

The other reason may be a lack of self-motivation. My coach provided motivation and support on the field.

There is another level of support required to challenge an athlete's desire to progress to a higher level. It's vital for athletes to have social interaction with their peers, and equally important for them to receive encouragement and support from their social environments—it may be a church family, a natural family, or a certain community. Our coach ensured that the athletes had the opportunity to sit and discuss the outcome of different events. Not everyone took advantage of the offer, but those who did were encouraged to keep up the good work. Others received advice on how to improve for the next event. Overall, the coach's advice was, "Never give up!"

We all experience strenuous situations along our Kingdom journey. Often we have experiences that make us feel as though we're going through a valley. Many followers of Christ refer to this as "the valley experience." In that place, we have to remind ourselves that, yes, every muscle in the body may ache, but this is not the end. This may look like a good place to sit and rest for a while, but if we call on the name of Jesus, He will release new strength.

The valley is a damp place, and yes, there are critters crawling down there. But let's remind ourselves that we are destined to receive the crown, not to relax with the critters. Motivate your mind. The journey is yet ahead.

On the other hand, when we finally crawl out of the valley, we have to climb along the slopes of the mountain. That image reminds me of an experience I had travelling to Rwanda two years ago. I quickly learned that I shouldn't look down while walking along the edges of a particular mountain. As we walked along, we had to ensure that we placed one foot directly in front of the other. If we did anything else, we might tumble down the side. It was a frightening possibility. So the idea was to remain focused on the journey, which would guarantee a person's safe arrival at their destination.

When we determine to acquire and develop new habits to discipline our lives of faith, many discouraging and deceptive thoughts come to derail us. But we must remain focussed.

Points to Ponder

- Where are you on the journey that you've been called to travel?
- Have you called on the name of Jesus when you sensed you were losing strength?

29

Self-Imposed Limitations

As we consider our endurance level, we cannot give up even though the journey is long and a bit exhausting. After all, you've invested a lot of energy to reach this level of the journey. God is aware that it's a strenuous and steep climb. He has confidence in your ability to move forward in His strength. Be encouraged. Connect with the Coach. Listen for His voice, for He is calling you by name. He has a sweet voice. The Coach of your soul recommends the following:

> *Therefore humble yourselves under the mighty hand of God, that He may exalt you in due time, casting all your care upon Him, for He cares for you.*
>
> —1 Peter 5:6–7

The runner must be willing to accept and undergo discipline, as this is the prerequisite for entering the race. It is part of the preparation. The coach is the one who often makes the final judgment and affirms an athlete's status. Further, the coach's mandate is to discern the level of activity that a runner feels confident to perform.

Under the umbrella of track and field, there are multiple disciplines. An athlete's ability is measured when specific skills are demonstrated. Athletes in this genre of sport are often skilled at multiple events. After their skills are identified, a mentor is assigned to provide in-depth guidance to help them solidify and improve in those disciplines.

In my capacity, I was slightly short in stature and encouraged to avoid the hurdles, the pole vault, and the high jump. Focusing on my stature merely created self-imposed limitations. With proper training, the obstacles that seemed challenging were actually attainable. Athletes who ventured into those events were specially gifted and had longer legs.

When we become believers and begin to walk in obedience to the will of God, we must function in the gifting and ability that have been identified within us. When we venture outside of that, we become a hindrance to ourselves and others. We must demonstrate our athleticism, which has been sanctioned by the Coach.

Because I knew where my challenges were—with regard to the hurdles, for example—I would admire the giftedness of my teammates and respectfully extend my admiration for their ability. This helped them feel motivated and affirmed in their gift.

30

Wearing the Right Garments

It is so important to understand the culture and environment of the race. It is equally important to be in the mindset of what happens in a race. When a runner isn't wearing the proper clothes, the garment may cause offense to other runners. As a member of the track team, we were all provided with special garments. We each had to pay an individual fee for these garments, which was part and parcel of accepting responsibility and demonstrating our accountability.

Each athlete had different garments for different purposes. For example, there were garments for practicing and exercising, garments for competing on the home track team, and garments for competitions held out of town. In fact, they were all colour-coded. If I showed up for practice wearing the competing-out-of-town garment, I would create an offense both to the coach as well as my team members. I would run the risk of having disciplinary actions taken against me. Some coaches would request the athlete pay a fine for such an offense.

One of the most important items is footwear. There are special shoes designed to mimic the feeling of having springs on your feet. When the shoes are on a runner's feet, a sense of readiness wells up inside them.

During practice sessions, there were times when I ran without shoes. Great damage was done to my feet as a consequence of this careless action. I developed heel spurs in both feet and had to have surgery to correct the problem. I became an advocate for other athletes on the subject of having appropriate footwear. Good footwear can eliminate the painful and traumatic experiences I had.

In Paul's epistle to the Ephesians, he encouraged them,

> *Therefore, put on every piece of God's armor so you will be able to resist the enemy in the time of evil. Then after the battle you will still be standing firm. Stand your ground, putting on the* belt *of truth and the body* armor *of God's righteousness. For* shoes, *put on the peace that comes from the Good News so that you will be fully prepared. In addition to all of these, hold up the* shield *of faith to stop the fiery arrows of the devil. Put on salvation as your* helmet, *and take the* sword *of the Spirit, which is the word of God.*
>
> —Ephesians 6:13–17, NLT (emphasis added)

Our Coach will not spur us forward into battle without proper covering. He has a much better perspective about the course we have to run than we do. He will not consent to us going into the race unprepared. When we wrap ourselves in the armour of God, it may appear, through the eyes of the flesh, that we don't stand a chance of winning. But through the eyes of faith, you will be at the finish line, waiting for the others and wondering, *What's taking them so long?*

It's a great privilege to be examined by the heavenly Coach. He examines us to check if we are properly clothed. He examines us to identify and rectify any part of the garment that needs to be restored or replaced. He examines us to ensure that we have the strength we need to complete the race. He will lovingly correct us so we can resemble the team player He has designed us to be.

David had a longing to be examined when he prayed:

Search me, O God, and know my heart;
test me and know my anxious thoughts.
Point out anything in me that offends you,
and lead me along the path of everlasting life.

—Psalm 139:23–24, NLT

From time to time, we all desire to hear feedback about ourselves. We don't always welcome criticism, especially when it comes in a condemning tone. Too often words of correction are given; rarely are words of affirmation. It's honourable to extend words of affirmation to those deserving of it.

King Solomon was very wise. He received his wisdom from the Lord, and he said: *"To learn, you must love discipline; it is stupid to hate correction"* (Proverbs 12:1, NLT). In his council about correction, he also said,

If you listen to constructive criticism,
you will be at home among the wise.

If you reject discipline, you only harm yourself;
but if you listen to correction, you grow in understanding.
Fear of the Lord teaches wisdom;
humility precedes honor.

—Proverbs 15:31–33, NLT

I recall having the same teacher in school for shorthand and typing. I thought she disliked me and wanted to pick on me all the time. All the *cool girls* sat at the back of the class, and naturally I considered myself cool so I would sit with them. However, I had an issue with my eyes and couldn't see the board from the back of the class. The teacher noticed it, and she always called me to sit in the vacant seat right next to her desk. I didn't want to sit in that seat, because anyone who sat there received the label of "teacher's pet." It meant a lot of teasing on the school grounds. Bullying was an issue and I would avoid recess by hiding out in the bathrooms.

Some of the girls from the cool girls group instigated fights with me because they considered me to be the teacher's pet. I hated that very much. I hated it even more when the teacher would nitpick my shorthand strokes and ask me to redo my work again and again.

The same thing happened in typing. We had those old typewriters and my fingers kept getting stuck in the spaces between the keys. It was torture. With my fingers all bruised up from the typewriter, I wasn't able to use my fountain pen to write as eloquently as she wanted.

Further, she addressed me by my last name, and that irritated me even more. I thought she sounded mean. At the end of the school year, I found out, through the guidance counsellor, that the teacher was pushing me because she recognized I had a talent, and she wanted to develop the skill she had identified.

There was another student in my classes who received high marks in shorthand and typing. The teacher initiated a competition that neither of us knew about. This other girl was not a teacher's pet; she was a member of the cool girls group.

At graduation, we both received a high achiever's award. It was very surprising to hear my name being called to receive an award. Shortly after that, we were both nominated to work at the only U.N. organisation in Canada that was accepting students with typing skills at a specified number of words per minute; we also had to have the ability to write and accurately transcribe business letters from shorthand notes.

When we receive corrections or chastisements, it's not always easy to accept them. It might seem harsh, and we might not see the reason for the correction. Our Coach permits corrections in our lives so we will grow in His grace and love. His intent is to uncover the truth about who we are in Him and to reveal the character of who He is in us. In the end, we will be awarded for the effort in completing the race.

My teacher intended to uncover our aptitude. Her efforts appeared a bit harsh, but in the end, the truth emerged. I recognized her character and acknowledged that she had not been such a mean teacher after all.

> FOR THE LORD CORRECTS THOSE HE LOVES, JUST AS A FATHER CORRECTS A CHILD IN WHOM HE DELIGHTS.

When we recognize and embrace the discipline of our heavenly Coach, we will know for sure that He loves and cares for us. We can examine this further by reading Proverbs 3:11–12:

> *My child, don't reject the Lord's discipline, and don't be upset when he corrects you. For the Lord corrects those he loves, just as a father corrects a child in whom he delights.* (NLT)

31

Dressed to Display His Glory

When we consider the process of clothing ourselves, we automatically see a representation of who we are. We become socially acceptable when we are clothed in the proper garment for the proper event.

Followers of Jesus assume a similar kind of grooming methodology. The clothes the Lord places upon us are garments that represent Him. We have to wear and display those garments with care.

Not many of us want to walk around in the latest and trendiest garments. We don't need to wear trendy clothes if we want to stand out in our social circles. However, if we wear the garment we are mandated to wear, we will be identified without even trying to become popular.

Let's put on *"love, joy, peace, longsuffering, kindness, goodness, faithfulness, gentleness, [and] self-control"* (Galatians 5:22–23). This is the ultimate and trendiest garment. When we wear it, we identify with the popular culture that prevails in the Kingdom of Heaven, Jesus' community. It's a garment that has received top rating; it is considered to be a garment of honour and praise.

32

Heckers Cause Distraction, Diversion, and Distortion

The whole idea of a race is to engage in competition. The supporters of different teams can be sitting right next to you in a stadium or arena. And there could be hecklers against your team. Their primary mandate is to disrupt your game and distract the player so he or she will lose focus. It is possible then that an athlete will become disengaged from the task at hand. It is also possible for an athlete to stumble, which could lead to interfering with other players.

Hecklers have one main function, and that is to keep the players on the opposing team from achieving their goal. They equip themselves with objects of diversion. Undisciplined players or athletes can easily fall victim and become casualties of the distraction. During the time of exercising and preparation, team members receive ongoing encouragement from their coach to maintain their focus. The ability to maintain focus inspires confidence and promotes maturity.

A segment of our training was to listen for the voice of our coach. His voice was immediately recognizable, and it was loud. If we obeyed any other voice during the competition, it would be noted and disciplinary actions would be handed out. Maintaining focus and listening for the coach's voice was central to completing and winning the race, reaching the goal, and obtaining the prize.

As followers of Christ, we have been selected to be members of His team. When we choose to join His team, we often experience warfare. In the same way, when we decide to participate in a sporting events, we must be aware of our surroundings in the arena, and especially be aware that there are both supporters and hecklers in attendance.

We must be able to identify the source of each voice and determine whether it is the recognizable voice that we have been trained to hear.

In our faith walk, there will be hecklers who equip themselves with negative words. They speak negative words to direct believers to take pathways away from the original one that was mapped out. Their words distort a believer's sense of hearing and vision.

Fear not. The Coach has taken possession of the seat in the auditorium of your heart. So let the games begin! While He is seated and positioned to enjoy the games, He whispers the words of Paul the Apostle, and asks this: *"What, then, shall we say in response to these things? If God is for us, who can be against us?"* (Romans 8:31, NIV)

33

Defying the Heckler

Our son was born prematurely. Many issues weighed him down as he was growing up. He had difficulties in school and some teachers thought he had hearing loss. He was tested by multiple specialists to determine the root cause of the problem. After much deliberation, they concluded that he had auditory processing disorder; he could lip-read but was not able to decipher between words that had similar sounds, like "sheep" or "sheet."

He had a very limited attention span and was only able to focus for about ten to fifteen minutes at a time. His teachers reported that he would tune out and find something more interesting to occupy his time. He was not a multitasker and could only retain a maximum of two instructions at once. The other students observed his behaviour and thought that if he could ignore the teacher and wander off to one corner of the classroom, maybe they could do it as well. He became a distraction to others.

The teachers came up with an idea. They developed a kind of contraption to help focus his attention. The teacher would wear a microphone around his or her neck like a necklace and my son would wear a headset resembling earmuffs. It was bright yellow and he hated to wear it; it drew a great deal of attention from the other students. It was so big that it was more like a helmet. As soon as the teacher observed that our son had exhausted his ten minutes of attention, he or she would say his name into the microphone or tap on the microphone, and it would echo in his ears to refocus his attention. That worked for a while, until he learned that he was the only one in school with such a gadget. We only learned that he wasn't wearing the equipment when his teacher called to inquire if he was sick because he hadn't been to his first class. At this point, he was in Grade Three. We had dropped him off at the early in-school daycare and his class officially started about an hour later. Somehow, he had discovered the janitor's room and one teacher found him sitting there. That was a sad time.

Following that experience, new tests were administered, and it was identified that he was developmentally deficient. Because of the disruptive behaviour he exhibited, they prescribed Ritalin. This popular drug was being prescribed for many boys during the mid- to late-eighties. A whole generation of boys was taking this medication to control their aggression.

Our son was given two doses per day. The teachers were aware of the medication and provided assistance to him during his lunch period.

After one month, our son became a different child. He was now very aggressive and we could no longer control him. His teachers observed the same thing. The Ritalin had the reverse effect on him and it was discontinued immediately. For the remainder of the schoolyear, he was provided with a tutor and a speech/language pathologist. He did well from that time on.

Hecklers disguise themselves in many ways; they are very creative. Their primary intention is to hinder our progress and set boulders in our path. These boulders can be invisible.

For years, the enemy used the challenges of our son to redirect and disrupt my focus. I spent many days, months, and years comparing and measuring his progress with others who were born around the same time. Naturally I always saw the problem rather than the potential. We had no support system to help us deal with the very real situation we were experiencing. As a mother, I internalized the problem and blamed myself for what was happening. I didn't share my inward pain for fear of judgment and finger-pointing. I didn't want to experience any further judgments in addition to the blame I already suited myself with.

There were days when I felt embarrassed and ashamed. Finally, I began to pray a different prayer: "God, I didn't make my son, You did. When he was born, we brought him to Your house and we presented him to You, so I am asking You to take care of him." It took a while, but eventually the heckler stopped whispering trash talk in my ears. And I was able continue on my journey toward the completion of my race.

About two years ago, we were sitting in front at a church meeting when a visiting minister, a prophet, said to me, "There is a rock of offence before you that wants you to trip and fall." I knew instantly what he meant. He continued, "Every stumbling block before you, they are cancelled in the name of Jesus. You will not stumble… you will no longer weep over your children. God is in control."

I take confidence in the fact that the Coach is aware of every offence and He stands in the position to remove them from my path so they will not hinder my race. He gives me the strength to defy the heckler and the taunting.

Points to Ponder

- Have you ever been at a game and heard advice shouted to the players by relatives and coaches? Have you ever done this yourself?
- Do you believe the athlete needs the advice?
- How should they determine which voice to focus on?

34

Lessons Learned

Many sport teams have athletes sitting on the bench, waiting to get the call or the tag to say "You're on next."

Why are they on the bench in the first place? There could be several reasons. One, the athlete is on the bench in case one of the regulars gets injured and is unable to take the team forward. Two, the benched athlete fails to carry out the instructions presented by the coach. In other words, he or she has an "it's my way, *not* your way" kind of attitude, so the coach has no choice but to apply the bench rule—sit. His intention is to bring the player into alignment with the objectives of the team. The hope is that the athlete will learn, through observation, from a different perspective.

35

Added Strength

He gives power to the weak, and to those who have no might He increases strength. Even the youths shall faint and be weary, and the young men shall utterly fall, but those who wait on the Lord shall renew their strength; they shall mount up with wings like eagles, they shall run and not be weary, they shall walk and not faint.

—Isaiah 40:29–31

I must have repeated this scripture about two hundred times. I went to sleep repeating the words, and when I woke up at midnight it was the first thing that came to my mind. Again, when I woke up in the morning, it was still there.

Finally, I said, "God, what would You like me know from this scripture?"

I heard Him say, "Regardless of the discipline you go through, or the training you have experienced, unless I deposit in you the strength to accomplish the race, all would be futile—it will not be successful. The eagle has the knowledge to soar high, allowing the wind to carry him up and forward. Without My intervention to release the wind under his wings, his strength would be non-existent."

Getting excited, I recalled that there were times when our team had entered the field and there was a sense of chaos all around. Crowds of people were everywhere, each group focused on different events. The atmosphere was charged with excitement. The activities had been predetermined. The conveners usually started right on schedule or even slightly before the fixed time. It was mandatory to wait and listen attentively for the call; the onus was on the athlete to hear the call.

God desires to take us away from the chaos. He wants to change the atmosphere where we've been for a while—*waiting*. For Him to change the atmosphere, we have to allow our spirits to soar above the crowd; we have to release the clutter from our minds and relinquish the activities that seem to gather in our environment and surrender the distractions we face.

When we are positioned for acceleration, the most important thing to surrender is our weakness. We need God's strength to empower us. When His strength is perfected in us, He receives the glory and we receive the reward. Only with His help can we accomplish His purpose and plan for our lives. It's a win-win situation.

36

Unmerited Favour and Divine Assistance

The Apostle Paul never failed to provide motivation to the believers. He attributes his ability to accomplish what he needed to the grace of God. According to Merriam-Webster's Dictionary, the word grace is defined as "unmerited divine assistance given [to] humans."[3] In other words, Paul did not earn or deserve God's favour; it was granted to him freely. And here, Paul acknowledged that he did not want to boast of any ability because he was the recipient of that divine assistance. Though he had a thorn in his flesh, Paul boasted solely in the work God had done in him. He had a thorn in his flesh. Some scholars have attempted to define what the thorn was. Paul did not disclose its identity to us. Rather, he said,

> *Concerning this thing I pleaded with the Lord three times that it might depart from me. And He said to me, "My grace is sufficient for you, for My strength is made perfect in weakness."*
>
> —2 Corinthians 12:8–9

---

3 Merriam-Webster.com, "Grace." Date of access: December 23, 2015 (http://www.merriam-webster.com/dictionary/grace).

I ended up with a thorn in my flesh: bone calcification. Some orthopaedic surgeons referred to the problem as plantar fasciitis or heel spurs. I had them on both feet. Eventually, I had to have them surgically removed.

As we mature, and while we are on the journey, certain situations will come to challenge us. The challenges are aimed at removing our eyes from the goal that's been set before us. The Coach may even be aware of it but withdraw from us, to test us and know what is in our hearts (2 Chronicles 32:31).

I had the spurs in my heels, but I never gave up. Through the pain in my heels, I was passionate enough to continue my training, my discipline, my running.

37

Positioned for Acceleration

The starting line of a race is also a place of inspection. The coach isn't the one doing the inspection; it is the game official. The official is now in charge, while the coach is positioned at the finish line.

One of the things the official does is inspect the athletes' attire. He examines their clothing to determine whether it is appropriate and within the rules. Next, the official examines the shoes. The required shoes are cleats, or shoes equipped with spikes at the bottom. The laces are also inspected to ensure they are secure.

The inspection is a way of showing respect to the other runners, of declaring that you have no intention of making them stumble during the race. You are declaring that you will not be a stumbling block or an offense.

The official has the names of each runner, with their corresponding number, to ensure that each one is positioned appropriately in the lane that is assigned to them. For the relay, the runners even have to run in a particular order.

When the inspection is complete, the official steps forward and says, "On your mark."

Many thoughts are going through the runner's head at this point. As the runner, much of the disciplinary training flashes before your eyes. One of the disciplines is to maintain your composure. You can decide to step aside if you do not feel composed, if you don't feel ready to go forward with the race. That indecision has consequences. It could disqualify the whole team. But it's easier to make the decision to step aside as opposed to having the official say, for example, "Runner number seven, lane two, please step aside." Those are devastating words and they are spoken quite often.

Just before the runner takes his or her mark, other incidents can cause him or her to lose composure. Other runners, possessing selfish intensions, can whisper negative or derogatory comments in their opponents' ears. These comment can be so insensitive and insulting that they have the potential to throw the runner off balance; the runner may feel demoralized, unable to concentrate on the goal. This type of intimidation is a tactic known as trash talk, and when it's used, the runner becomes agitated and may entertain the risk of encroaching on the boundaries of other athletes. They lose confidence. When the opponent talks trash, the official is unaware of it. The enemy positions himself in such a way that it is not apparent when a violation is taking place. Can you visualize this?

Join me as we, through the eye of the Spirit of God, disarm and disallow these types of actions spiked with malicious intent.

The Coach is fully aware when evil plots are hurled against those He positions for acceleration in His Kingdom purposes. He stands ready to foil and frustrate the plans of the enemy. The Scriptures tell us that *"God has not given us a spirit of fear, but of power and of love and of a sound mind"* (2 Timothy 1:7).

Often, we become intimidated by our surroundings. We permit fear and timidity to take hold of us. In the long run, we become stuck because we beat ourselves up over our inabilities. When we give in to fear, we forget that we have been empowered by faith. The result is that we fail to release the message of hope and freedom to the captive, and miss out on the intended blessing.

Paul was encouraging Timothy not the give permission for fear to take hold of him. He needed to be in control of the spirit of power within him. He needed to exercise the love of God to display the grace of God. He needed to have soundness of mind to release the measure of God's grace to those to whom he was sent. Timothy was a young man and perhaps didn't have enough confidence to complete the tasks that were assigned to him. He hadn't fully developed the art of maintaining his composure by laying aside his fears.

The official says, "Set."

After a five-second count, the run gun goes off, and the race begins.

38

Passing the Baton

My coach would get very excited for a particular event: the relay. Four runners accomplished the relay race. Each runner had to complete one hundred meters. The coach was so passionate about this game that his passion carried over into the way he trained the team. He coordinated the four runners based on their ability or speed. When he used this strategy, it was guaranteed that we would win. He arranged the team in this order:

- Runner 1 was the one with the slowest time.
- Runner 2 was the one with the fastest time.
- Runner 3 was the one with the second fastest time.
- Runner 4 was the one with the second slowest time.

Other teams couldn't comprehend our strategy. It left other coaches scratching their heads, trying to figure out why we were successful. As team members, we were cautioned not to disclose our strategy. After all the years that have passed, they must have figured it out by now. It was wonderful to see the joy on the coach's face when we were declared the winner. The joy was contagious.

For the relay, runners had to display their multitasking skills. There was a process of transferring and receiving the baton. Both actions were dependent on the dominant hand of each runner. For example, as a right-handed runner, I received the baton with my left hand, but I had to be aware of the dominant hand of the runner to whom I would transfer the baton. We had both left-handed and right-handed athletes on the team. So when the transfer of the baton was complete, with the proper synchronization, the coach was exhilarated.

One imperative element of the transfer is that there is a specified passing zone on the course. The recipient must be aware of the number of strides to take within that zone. The recipient cannot be looking backward while attempting to accelerate. Both the individual transferring and the one receiving must be completely aware of each other's abilities and strengths. If the transfer of the baton is not complete within the specified zone, the team is automatically disqualified, and severe consequences are applied against the responsible team member.

The possibility also existed for a team member to cross the paths of other runners; they could trip and fall. That one error could create a domino effect and the potential for multiple injuries. When all lanes were busy—called "runner traffic"—the race was susceptible to incidents. As athletes, we had to be cautious.

Our coach demonstrated his joy and exhilaration when he saw his passion for the relay event mimicked in the runners he had trained. His reaction was to kiss all ten of his fingers and throw his hands in the air.

For coaches and mentors, it is a delight when a student or pupil expresses their gratitude for the manner in which they have been guided towards success. The mentor experiences irreplaceable pride. This is not the sort of pride that surges through the head of an individual with notions of self-righteousness and personal grandeur, but rather it's wrapped in humility. Not many individuals can separate pride and humility, making them work together so God gets the glory.

In our daily lives, we are running a race. Having the knowledge of the Word of God will point us in the direction to the finish line. One of the psalms says, "*I will sing of the mercies of the Lord forever; with my mouth will I make known Your faithfulness to all generations*" (Psalm 89:1).

I was given the mandate to use my mouth to transfer the Word of God and declare His faithfulness to those in the generations He has called me to. Transferring the Word is like transferring the baton. I cannot hold on to it. If I do that, I risk bringing the race to a halt. The whole plan of completing the race could be terminated if I give allowance to pride and self-centredness. It's insubordinate to hold on to the baton when I know it should be transferred to others. There are longings and eagerness in the hearts of those who have also been trained, who have gone through the discipline in anticipation of becoming a participant in the race.

We will readily agree with the psalm that says, "*Your word is a lamp to my feet and a light to my path*" (Psalm 119:105).

39

Voice of Authority

I had a grandma Lois in my life. She had already completed her race and was waiting for her prize. Lois was sure to transfer, with authority, the words of the Lord into my life on a regular basis. She recognized each time I wavered in my level of obedience in listening to the Lord and releasing the words He had spoken to my heart.

Lois sat quietly in the assembly, but she was always veiled in God's glory and surrounded by His presence. During our praise and worship gatherings, she constantly had a sense when the Spirit of God released a word. As a family, we habitually sat behind Grandma Lois in the meetings.

There were times when I received a word. I was hesitant to speak it, because I felt a bit timid. Or I thought that perhaps my mind was playing tricks on me. In that period of waiting, Lois would begin to speak—and she would speak the exact words that had been in my heart and mind.

When this happened, she wouldn't hesitate to release a reprimand with a voice of authority: "Why have you chosen to disobey the Lord by withholding the word He has given to you to release?" The reprimand was often directed at me or my beloved. She loved us dearly and we never felt destroyed or dismantled by her. She was merely providing the guidance we needed and making sure that we were the head and not the tail in regards to the gifts God had deposited in our lives. There was no getting around Grandma Lois, and that was a demonstration of her position in the Lord Jesus Christ. We had to promise that we would walk in obedience next time.

In my eyes, Grandma Lois carried the baton and effectively transferred it to many others in my generation. She has completed her leg of the race and has been positioned in anticipation of her prize.

Some may ask, "So when does the race ends?" Well, it doesn't end until the final runner crosses the finish line.

In 2 Timothy 1:3–7, we learn that Timothy also had a grandmother like Lois. She was used by God to transfer the baton of faith to him. Through time, Paul the Apostle became a mentor and coach who guided Timothy farther in the race that he was commissioned to run.

My coach was always aware of the runner in the last position. Based on the hours of practice, he was able to focus on his timer and discern the exact time the final runner would arrive at the finish line. That was precision. He maintained his confidence that he had transferred the baton—the training and discipline—to his team. He stood in pride and echoed, "That's my team." It was great to see the joy on his face. The unity and camaraderie displayed there were priceless and always served as motivation and enthusiasm for the next event. The coach knew that receiving the prize was contingent upon all runners completing the race.

Points to Ponder

- Do you know where you have been positioned?
- Have you identified your mentor?

40

Transfer to Transform

In an earlier section, I recounted a vision in which a dove descended with a scroll. This is a beautiful symbol of what the Spirit of God is uncovering in our lives. The dove came with this message: "Teach them what I have taught you."

There is another important image here. The scroll is a representation of the baton that is used in the relay race. This transfer must take place in order to complete the race to which we have been called. The knowledge of the word is central to accomplishing the race in anticipation of obtaining the prize.

As we are commissioned to run the race and transfer the baton, we must preach the Gospel. Praise and honour go to the throne of God when we hand over the baton. We feel an immediate sense of accomplishment. The runner immediately says within him or herself, "I have done it." The cheers that erupt from the spectators provides added motivation.

When we speak the Word and release the message of the Gospel to those who are waiting to receive it, the angels rejoice. There is rejoicing in heaven.

41

Stirred by Unshakable Passion

As I recount my participation in the race, a passion is stirred up in me. It is amazing that after all this time, I'm still not able to shake it. I'm not sure when the flow of adrenalin will dissipate. It's a demonstration to me that when the love of God is released in our hearts, it's not easily removed. If I were to explain the supernatural impartation of love, that's how I would describe it: it is an unshakable passion. God has made a runner of me. It is a part of my DNA.

When we take our place to commence the race, positioned for acceleration, like Paul we can acknowledge our weakened humanity but take courage as we receive strength in the confidence that Christ provides for us: "*For when I am weak, then I am strong*" (2 Corinthians 12:10)

Points to Ponder

- What do you consider to be a part of your DNA?
- What specific characteristics do you possess to demonstrate that you are fearfully and wonderfully made?

42

Hold on to the Promises

God's love for me is immense. It was unheard of to visit my parents and not attend church on Sunday mornings. During one visit to a church I had never been to before, there were some special meetings with visiting pastors. I walked into the meeting and found a seat about five rows back.

Five minutes after settling into my seat, the pastor stood up to deliver the message for the day. She read her scripture, taken from the book of Revelation, speaking of one of the churches mentioned there.

Suddenly, she began walking off the platform and heading into the crowd.

Where is she going? I asked myself.

She kept coming closer to where I was sitting, all the while continuing to speak.

I realized that she was coming in my direction.

No one anticipated what she was about to say and do. However, she came directly to where I was sitting—with her finger pointing at me—and repeated three times: "Hold on to the promises of God."

She said nothing else. She walked back to the podium and continued her message.

It is so wonderful to know that God deals with each one of us as individuals. He knows where we are and when we have a longing in our hearts to hear Him speak. I was going through some stuff at the time and was seeking God's intervention. Actually, I was attempting to tell God what to do and when to do it, and if He didn't do it I was simply not going back to church. That was my attitude. I wanted Him to fix those people who had offended me, and if He didn't… well, no more church for me.

Can you imagine that I was giving attitude to God? How many of us have done that?

Walking away from the church would have meant giving up on the promises He has ordained for me to claim. As we mature in faith, whether God speaks to us—often in dramatic ways, like he used the pastor to do—or whether He is silent, He is still God, and we cannot control Him with our personalities and attitudes. He brings us through the tough stuff in our lives and reassures us that we must walk in unshakable confidence. He supports us with His provision and strength to move us forward.

"HOLD ON TO THE PROMISES OF GOD."

43

Kingdom Culture

Immediately following graduation from high school, I started working. I worked with an organization that is a member of the United Nations. One of the mandates of this organization is to develop standards and recommended practices for international airports, taking into consideration every country and region of the world.

As I became immersed in that environment, I noticed the culture of high diplomacy. It was also clear that the culture captured a sense of formality. The formal setting existed because high-level decisions occurred. It was in that milieu that I met three former prime ministers of Canada: Pierre Elliott Trudeau, Jean Chretien, and Paul Martin. I also met the former U.N. Secretary General Kofi Anan, as well as astronauts Marc Garneau and Roberta Bondar.

The culture was so formal that everyone, apart from my immediate colleagues, was addressed as Your Excellency, Doctor, Mr., Mrs., and Captain. Personally, I owned two sets of clothes—formal and semi-formal. It was a bit hilarious that I worked in the organization for more than eighteen years and I'd only every owned one pair of jeans.

After eighteen years steeped in that culture, the Lord transitioned us to Ottawa where I accepted work in another culture, the federal government. This was a more informal setting and the training I'd received in the formal environment was not a requirement in my new and relaxed environment. Managers and supervisors didn't desire the honour and formality; they preferred first names. It took me a while to adapt to the new culture, but I did, with some training.

In the physical, there is one level of dignitaries I have yet to meet. I have not met the Queen of England, nor has an invitation been extended for me to meet her. In the supernatural, I have encountered the King of Heaven. He is divinely addressed as "Your Majesty, King of Kings and Lord of Lords." His arms extend to all who enter before Him as He releases His authority to ratify whatever needs to be ratified in the Spirit.

In the ambiance of Kingdom culture, we are guaranteed to experience His love beyond measure. In the environment and atmosphere of the King's presence, there is freedom. In Kingdom culture, the dress code at all times is garments of praise. It is a garment with the flexibility to dance, jump, run, kneel, and bow down. That is the culture of His Kingdom.

44

Identification

When we were scheduled for a race away from home, it was mandatory for the coach to take along the flag that represented the school. If the identification was missing, we couldn't register in the event. My coach was always ready with his credentials. Only once have I encountered a team that had to sit on the sidelines, unable to participate, because the coach didn't bring the team's credentials and identification.

The Coach provides familiarization training in the presence of diplomats and dignitaries. It is mandatory preparation for disciples—for commissioning and positioning. Disciples are sent out as ambassadors and representatives, and must ensure that they possess credentials that are honourable to the name of Jesus Christ.

One of the greatest indicators to ensure we possess the proper credentials and carry the right identification is the love we display for each other.

We simply declare that Christ is the awesome Coach and His desire is for us to be trained and equipped with all we need to be successful on the journey to the end of the race.

When we enroll to begin a race, we may lack the confidence to run in an unfamiliar environment. However, we have been trained to operate in an atmosphere of supernatural confidence and display the credentials provided by the Coach of coaches.

45

Other Territories

Paul ran his race in several territories and among multiple people groups such as Galatians, Ephesians, Philippians, Colossians, and Thessalonians. Many people were observing him to see how he performed in the race he was called to run. Not only did he run the race among them, he was sure to provide motivation to them as they engaged in the race.

46

Maximize the Capacity of Your Tent

God wanted to enlarge my territory. He brought me out of one situation and placed me into another so I could learn about expansion. It is always God's intention that we take hold of His purpose for our lives, seeing our lives from a higher perspective and through wider lenses.

I had to learn the physical dimension of the grounds along which my journey would take me. From that perspective, I had to claim, by His inspiration of faith, every territory and every place that my feet would travel for His Kingdom.

That act of claiming territory was validated when I was invited to lead a local chapter of an international women's ministry. It was my pleasure to do so, because I would get to promote the business of the Kingdom and participate in the race.

During my commissioning to minister in that capacity, the outgoing leader presented me with a tent peg. She offered no explanation, but I knew that it was a symbolic representation of the expansion the Lord was about to do.

When we align ourselves to walk in obedience, we do things for reasons that are not immediately apparent to us. The presentation of the tent peg was an act of obedience. This would become clear when I viewed it through the lens of faith.

God knows the exact reason I was not presented with a bouquet of flowers. When we receive the promises of God, nothing can hinder their fulfillment in our lives. You see, if I had received flowers, they would have wilted and died within a couple of days. Years later, I still have the tent peg. It serves as a reminder of His promises to me and the ongoing intention God has to enlarge my territory.

When we set out to run, the path ahead may appear narrow. But the path gets wider with each step we take toward the finish line. We get a sense of expansion both from our eyes and our feet. Our vision is extended and the borders of our territory become enlarged. That is an awesome picture of what God wants us to understand from His perspective.

In the Word, we read,

> *Enlarge the place of your tent, and let them stretch out the curtains of your dwellings; do not spare; lengthen your cords, and strengthen your stakes. For you shall expand to the right and to the left…*
>
> —Isaiah 54:2–3

Let me encourage you to hold on to the promise (or tent peg) that He has presented to you. It will serve as a marker to identify the distance you have travelled, and it will be a testimony to the width of the territory you must embrace. Along the journey, the tent peg will become a reminder of His faithfulness to move you toward your destination.

Most recently, I was awakened in the early morning with this thought: *To maximize the capacity of your tent, you must enlarge the border.*

47

Be Careful Not to Disqualify Yourself

I sat at my computer early one morning when I got to work, unsure why I couldn't focus on the tasks I had scheduled for the day. After having my coffee, I was able to muster up enough energy to review my agenda and get an overview of what would set the pace for the day.

Usually, I have a cup of coffee each morning. I pick one up before I arrive in the office. But it would be unwise of me to attribute my daily strength to the cup of coffee. I know that my strength comes from the Lord. I know that He is my dependency.

Yet I have found myself relying on that cup of coffee. I had to break the habit when the Lord so gently brought it to my attention. I realized that I had to be careful to make the proper declaration regarding my source of strength and my dependency.

So on this particular morning, after having coffee, me and my colleagues were advised that a particular co-worker would be in to work a bit later than usual; she had a first-things-first situation going on in her family.

When she arrived, she was so excited. She had spent some time with her family for an early morning celebration. The party had taken place at the airport, she announced. She was anxious to tell the exciting news that her family member (a distant cousin), who had been a participant in the Olympics, had just come home. He hadn't won a medal, but the family gathered together to meet him at the airport and celebrate his homecoming. That's a beautiful expression of unity. From her excitement, one would think that she was the one who had participated in the games.

My colleague's story simply reminded me of how we, as children of God, should be so eager to demonstrate His love and care for one another. If anyone is rejoicing, we should all rejoice, and if anyone is crying, we should be willing to cry with them (Romans 12:15).

As I continued my work, my thoughts drifted back to the joys I had experienced in the races. At times I longed to share the joys and excitement with other members of my family and friends. I reminisced about how awesome it would have been for me to share with them the good news that I had occasionally received first place honours. I was at work, though, so I couldn't drift off into those thoughts for a prolonged period. The Spirit and presence of the Lord are with us at all times, and I immediately heard Him say: "Be careful that you do not disqualify yourself."

I had to inquire what He meant about disqualifying myself. I began to converse with the Lord, and He began to show me visions—as though I was sitting in a movie theatre. He showed me the crowds of angels who were standing by as I ran the race. He illuminated the pathway that He had designed for me to run. There were caution lights flashing; they pointed directly at the prize positioned at the end of the path. If I shifted my gaze to the left or to the right, the lights would shift and highlight the danger of overrunning the boundary lines. How devastating it would be to lose out on the prize that way.

"It is extraordinarily important to avoid disqualification," He said.

He also showed me that I was seeking the approval of men and women rather than seeking His approval. It wasn't necessary for me to spend time glancing backward; it was imperative that I spend time looking forward.

When I came back to reality, I was still sitting at my desk. There are some experiences we have in life when, suddenly, the light goes on. For me, this was such a moment. Since my childhood days, I'd had the desire to receive the applause of others. Positive reinforcement hadn't often been spoken to me.

So from time to time, the need to receive a pat on the shoulder emerges. It is part and parcel of the old nature elevating itself in my heart—and in my life. I am grateful that the Coach cautions me to be careful that I do not disqualify myself.

Paul didn't want to be disqualified based on self-centeredness or prideful ambitions. He had his eyes focused on the prize that was eternal rather than one that would tarnish. He was determined to model the posture of the athlete, destined to receive the prize. He posed this question:

> *Do you not know that those who run in a race all run, but one receives the prize? Run in such a way that you may obtain it. And everyone who competes for the prize is temperate in all things. Now they do it to obtain a perishable crown, but we for an imperishable crown. Therefore I run thus: not with uncertainty. Thus I fight: not as one who beats the air. But I discipline my body and bring it into*

subjection, lest, when I have preached to others, I myself should become disqualified.

—1 Corinthians 9:24–27

As we run, we must run in consideration of other team members. The runners who went before us had to be watchful that they didn't cross the lines that could hamper their race and cause their disqualification. Likewise, vigilance is key. I have to ensure that I run within the boundaries or risk the disqualification of my team members.

48

Another Phase of Transition

I was getting agitated at the fact that our house wasn't selling. We had so many visitors going through our house, and it was starting to feel creepy. We had to manicure the house to immaculate perfection and walk away for the viewers to come in. Often, we didn't receive any feedback from the selling agent. When we did receive comments, it went something like "Your house is very clean." Well, yes. I cleaned it. Certainly the potential buyer wouldn't expect that I would leave the house in a mess. I was looking for positivity, but I wasn't really getting it. I saw these as unnecessary comments and I discounted them.

I was getting impatient with the agent until God turned the light on, so to speak. It literally felt like sitting in a dark or dimly lit room until someone came in and turned the light on. Only when the light goes on do you realize that you've been sitting in the dark. He wanted me to become aware that He had granted the time for me to step into a new season of the plan He had preordained. A very short verse says, *"In Your light we see light"* (Psalm 36:9). Jesus also declared in John 8:12, *"I am the light of the world. He who follows Me shall not walk in darkness, but have the light of life."* It is wonderful to give Him permission to turn the light on for us and in us.

49

A Tranquil Place

I had been off work for two months. About two weeks into this period, I began to sense that it was time to write my book—an idea that had been circulating in my heart for some time. Throughout the years, I have dismissed the idea of writing a book. Now I could no longer dismiss it.

We anticipated that the house would sell in a short period of time. I enjoyed the tranquillity that I'd come to experience from being in our very quiet neighbourhood. Each day, I had a different experience with nature, God's creation.

On the property we had regular and daily visits from animals such as foxes, deer, coyotes, rabbits, racoons, turkeys, turtles, snakes, frogs, birds of multiple species, squirrels, chipmunks, geese, and finally a swan who was named Ramon by the community. He impersonated a goose for many months. When Ramon first arrived, he began to claim territory. In other words, he released an ear-piercing sound; many began to wonder why he was doing that.

We realized later that Ramon was communicating with the other geese, telling them that he was there and if they wanted to swim, they were to enter at their own risk. This behaviour went on for weeks. Finally, the sound subsided and geese started to arrive in droves. Eventually, they were all friends. It was amazing to see the hundreds of geese—and among them this one white swan.

Nearing the end of summer, members of the community thought that Ramon should be captured and brought back to a sanctuary where he could socialize with other birds of his own kind. That was not a good idea. I believe Ramon had been directed there in the first place; he hadn't come through human intervention.

Ramon was captured and was gone a mere eighteen hours when news hit social media that Ramon had passed away. It was concluded by the neighbourhood that Ramon died of a broken heart when he was separated from his friends that bore another type of feather. Ramon was willing to stand up (so to speak) and be counted. It hadn't been an issue for him that his feathers were of another type; he hadn't allowed the fact that his feathers were different to stop him from becoming a part of the community of geese.

Ramon's story exactly describes the position God wants us to take. He takes us out of our comfort zones and positions us into another environment where He desires for us to function.

We are to release the sounds He has given to us to release. That sound must be communicated with His authority and power.

It is often difficult to transition into a new place, but He will supply the strength we need to succeed there. We cannot depend on human intervention unless God has authorized it. Human intervention will only bring trauma and death to the plans and purposes He has for us. When He calls and positions us in the environment where He wants us to display the skills He has equipped us with, He also provides the operational authority—the wisdom and knowledge—for us to move forward.

In this environment of peace and tranquillity, the Lord turned the light on and revealed to my heart that my book needed to be completed. The tranquillity and love that I had come to experience was part and parcel of His provision. So I contacted a publisher and received a deadline.

The light kept getting brighter and brighter, highlighting the fact that God had a specific assignment for me in this season of my life. Only after I accomplished the task He had given me to do—from that place of tranquillity—would the transition be fully realized. Jeremiah 29:11–13 states,

> *For I know the thoughts that I think toward you, says the Lord, thoughts of peace and not of evil, to give you a future and a hope. Then you will call upon Me and go and pray to Me, and I will listen to you. And you will seek Me and find Me, when you search for Me with all your heart.*

What an incredible announcement of the plan God has declared over our lives. The main ingredient of this plan is simple obedience. Personally, I've had to come to the end of myself and say, "Okay, God, what is the next thing?"

One of the prophetic words we received prior to leaving for Ottawa was that He had already provided whatever we may need. His provisions have been incredible.

One of the churches that was established here in Ottawa grew out of our home. Often when we had our Sunday morning worship, we had to move furniture (the kitchen table and other bulky items) outside on the deck to make room for people to sit. Some were only able to find a spot on the kitchen counter, next to the sink. We removed pictures and wall hangings to project song lyrics on the walls.

The church consisted of students from several universities, such as Trent University in Peterborough, Toronto University, the University of Ottawa, and Carleton University. There were also some students who joined us from Algonquin College.

> HE HAD ALREADY PROVIDED WHATEVER WE MAY NEED.

We experienced miracles and healings. Some were healed from depression and emotional torment. Others were healed from intestinal disorders. Some were released from the bondages of drug addiction. Others experienced mental health conditions due to the pressure imposed on them to be high achievers. They were not only high achievers academically; they were also high achievers in the realm of the spirit.

That was an explosive time in God. The word was getting out that something marvellous was happening in Ottawa. Those who came from Peterborough and Toronto would drive for three or four hours to arrive for a 10:30 a.m. meeting. That is something to marvel about. Even today, I have fond memories of the eagerness that took hold of those young people. It had to be a supernatural hunger and thirst for the presence of God that He divinely deposited within them. My beloved and I were the seniors among them.

After each meeting, a meal was provided. There was always something in the oven during the winter months. And in the spring or summer, the barbeque was fired up. Finally, when we observed there was standing room only in our large family room, kitchen, and dining room, we decided that it was time to rent a community building. And so we did.

The church began to grow because of the miracles that were happening and the unity being displayed. The students began to bring their friends and told others what was happening. Regularly, after the meeting someone wanted to be baptized, so the bathtub always had to be clean. We had to establish student cell groups, and even during weekday house meetings (held in student dorms and apartments) people were getting saved and being baptized.

As I write these things, I am reminded that these experiences mirrored those that happened in the book of Acts during the early church. They were due to the provision of the Lord, just as it was prophesied. The Scriptures say,

> *So shall My word be that goes forth from My mouth; it shall not return to Me void, but it shall accomplish what I please, and it shall prosper in the thing for which I sent it. For you shall go out with joy, and be led out with peace; the mountains and the hills shall break forth into singing before you, and all the trees of the field shall clap their hands.*
>
> —Isaiah 55:11–12

I fondly recall one particular student who, week after week, came to the meeting wearing the same clothes. I observed this from the time we were having house meetings, and it continued on to when we met at the community centre. God had healed her of depression and anointed her voice with an angelic tone. She was encouraged to be part of the worship team.

One Sunday when it was time to start the worship segment of the meeting, I stood and began worshipping with my eyes closed. I attempted to position my heart and mind to worship. I couldn't see the Lord, though; I kept seeing images of this young lady. I had previously observed that she appeared to be losing some weight. So I opened my eyes and tried to redirect my gaze, to focus on something else. Needless to say, it wasn't working.

Finally, I surrendered and prayed, *God, what do You want to show me about this young lady?*

I've come to realize that it is virtually impossible to worship the Lord wholeheartedly when you set out to worship Him half-heartedly. My thoughts were not fully centred on Him. It was preoccupied with something regarding the young lady in front of me.

The Lord answered me and said, "You need to provide this young lady with some money."

I swallowed deeply and sat down. But I got back to my feet because I didn't want to draw attention to myself.

I started to sing, but no sound came out. I was just lip-syncing, and I thought doing that would keep me out of trouble; it would keep others from noticing that I was really having an encounter with the Lord. That was exercising bad behaviour.

Subconsciously, it placed me in the arena of self-deception. I deceived myself into believing that God wasn't a speaking God.

When Jesus spoke to the disciples about being the Good Shepherd, He said, "My sheep know my voice" (John 10:14, paraphrased). That statement delivers a brilliant model for the type of intimate relationship that must exist between the sheep and its shepherd.

While I was still pretending (pretending to sing, pretending not to hear), I was processing what I had heard from the Lord. But I didn't act on what I heard. When I agreed to demonstrate a heart of obedience, my posture for worship became centred on Christ Jesus. My spirit came into agreement with the psalm that reads: "*Bless the Lord, O my soul; and all that is within me, bless His holy name!*" (Psalm 103:1) Another psalm declares, "*Create in me a clean heart, O God, and renew a steadfast spirit within me*" (Psalm 51:10).

Immediately following the meeting, I pulled this young lady aside and we spoke privately and confidentially. She informed me that following her conversion, she had stopped taking medications for depression, and as a result of not taking them, she lost some weight. I was so proud of her. Her birthday was fast approaching and she prayed that God would provide her with the funds to revamp her wardrobe.

I nearly broke down—not with pity, but with joy—because the Lord was downloading His blessings upon her. There was more to come and she didn't know it yet.

She also advised me that her friend was getting married and had asked her to be a part of the wedding party. She wasn't sure how she was going to do that because she had depleted her savings on medications and she hadn't yet accumulated enough funds to purchase all the items she needed for the wedding.

I embraced her and whispered in her ear the amount of money the Lord had asked me to release to her. She wept. But I cautioned her to keep the information to herself. She respected my request, and all was well.

It turned out that we, my beloved and I, were invited to the same wedding a few months later. This young lady didn't hesitate to approach me. We embraced, and then she twirled around to model all the items she had purchased. My heart rejoiced. It was a simple demonstration of the beauty and blessings of God. He truly is worthy of our worship.

It didn't stop there. It turned out that her hometown was about five hours away by car. She had, in fact, shared the information about our gift with her parents. They also called to express their thanks and appreciation. They didn't have enough words to express their feelings.

We were surprised one day when the doorbell rang at home. The couple at the door identified themselves as the parents of this young lady. Oh my. My heart skipped a beat because I thought something was wrong. The truth is that they had driven for five hours to come to Ottawa because they longed to be introduced to the people who had showed such extravagant kindness to their daughter.

The glory belongs to God. The magnitude of His provision was echoed in a song some years earlier, saying, "He has already provided." We are blessed to be a blessing.

Points to Ponder

- When we enter into the presence of God and endeavour to worship, do we worship Him out of duty or desire?
- What is the difference between worshiping for duty or desire?

50

Reaching the Finish Line

During training, my coach insisted that I train alongside two long-distance runners. I was a sprinter. The dictionary defines a sprint as: "a race over a short distance at a very fast speed" or "to run or go very fast for a short distance."[4]

It was difficult to keep up with those runners, especially because they were so tall. It took three of my strides to make one of theirs. I didn't know what the coach was thinking. He just kept saying, "It's good for you to run with them."

At the end of those practice runs, I often found myself flat on my back, somewhere on the field, trying to recuperate from the exhaustion. We would have five minutes to rest, and then we were off again. It was challenging.

I thought the coach was trying to push me hard enough so I would quit the team.

That wasn't the case at all.

It is evident now that the purpose was to build endurance. The coach endeavoured to establish in me a level of determination,

---

4 Merriam-Webster.com, "Sprint." Date of access: December 23, 2015 (http://www.merriam-webster.com/dictionary/sprint).

endurance, and confidence. He saw the potential that was there and wanted to build on it.

We don't always see the strengths we have and how those strengths contribute to our personal growth and development. More often than not, it takes someone outside of ourselves to recognize or notice our potential. The thoughts I had for myself weren't necessarily positive, yet the coach's were very positive.

Ongoing training is needed in this area of my life. I need to exercise patience with myself as I develop the godly endurance required to run my race. The Coach of my soul says,

> *For My thoughts are not your thoughts, nor are your ways My ways… For as the heavens are higher than the earth, so are My ways higher than your ways, and My thoughts than your thoughts.*
>
> —Isaiah 55:8–9

I don't know if you're familiar with the very popular children's book series entitled "Where's Waldo?" It provided hours and hours of entertainment for my boys. Those were the days before the entrance of technology into our lives, with all the gadgets available now. The object was to find Waldo who, though he was dressed in very specific and recognizable clothing, was hidden among objects in locations where many different activities were happening. The children were encouraged to exercise patience and endurance in order to find Waldo.

It was interesting to observe my sons as they expressed joy and excitement when they discovered Waldo's hiding place.

As we envision the finish line, through the lens of faith, we will see that there are thousands who have completed the race before us. They are waiting on the sidelines, anticipating our arrival. When we see them standing there, we may wonder why they haven't claimed their prize. Let's remind ourselves: we are a team. Every member must reach the end before the prizes are handed out. Hebrews 11:39–40 says,

> *All these people earned a good reputation because of their faith, yet none of them received all that God had promised. For God had something better in mind for us, so that they would not reach perfection without us.* (NLT)

To obtain the prize, we need to set our sights on the finish line. We have to devote the time for exercise. With patience and endurance, we train our spiritual bodies. We have to be willing to tolerate the discipline the Coach offers. He only recommends the training He is familiar with, for He knows the workouts that will condition the muscles we will use during the race. He has proven that these workouts are good for us.

51

Running a Different Race: It Is My Journey

I want to encourage us all to run the race with strength. This strength comes when we practice with long-distance runners and build up the endurance required to complete the race. When we join as a team under the Coach's authority, we are conditioning ourselves to *run a different race*—for then it becomes our journey. The reward at the end of the journey will bring joy and excitement.

Desire Women's Ministry

Desire Women's Ministry is focused on the expository teaching of the Word of God and discovering the uncompromising truths that it contains.

Visit us at www.desirechristianwomensministry.com to learn more about the ministry and events, and to connect with Sonia Henry.